STUDY GUIDE

Brinton, Christopher and Wolff

A History of
Civilization
Prehistory to 1715

Fifth Edition

JOSEPH W. INK
Cleveland State University

Prentice-Hall, Inc., Englewood Cliffs, New Jersey

Printed in the United States of America

10 9 8 7 6 5 4 3 2 1

ISBN: 0-13-389833-4

PRENTICE-HALL INTERNATIONAL, INC., London
PRENTICE-HALL OF AUSTRALIA PTY. LIMITED, Sydney
PRENTICE-HALL OF CANADA, LTD., Toronto
PRENTICE-HALL OF INDIA PRIVATE LIMITED, New Delhi
PRENTICE-HALL OF JAPAN, INC., Tokyo
PRENTICE-HALL OF SOUTHEAST ASIA PTE, LTD., Singapore

CONTENTS

Purpose and Uses of the Study Guide

If History is defined as everything Mankind has ever said or done or thought, then a college freshman about to undertake a study of "Western Civilization" would seem to face an almost impossible task. Even if we entrust several professional historians with the duty of condensing all of civilization into three volumes, the student still has the monumental job of trying to learn everything in the book, of plotting to outguess his teacher, or of using some meaningful method of figuring out what is important and sifting it out from what is less important. Since most freshmen take a heavy load of tough beginning courses and have little experience in separating the vital from the trivial, they can easily end up in a guessing game in which the stakes are far too high for comfortable or happy digestion of the joys as well as the discipline of the study of history.

This Study Guide is an attempt to provide the student with help from an experienced teacher on how to read the textbook, how to organize the material in some understandable manner, and how to anticipate possible questions and plan intelligent answers for examinations. This Study Guide to a History of Civilization is intended to be used with Volume I of A History of Civilization, Fifth Edition, by Crane Brinton, John B. Christopher, and Robert Lee Wolfe.

The Study Guide will follow the Civilization textbook chapter by chapter and will be organized to deal with each chapter in several different ways:

1) A TOPIC OUTLINE of each chapter in the textbook;

2) A MAP EXERCISE or, in a few cases, exercises;

3) A list of TERMS, PEOPLE, AND EVENTS from the chapter and;

4) A group of SAMPLE QUESTIONS which are designed to be typical of what might be asked over the material from the chapter.

-1-

These items are designed to help students in a typical freshman survey course in Western Civilization and are so aimed at that level, but advanced students taking the same course should find the Study Guide useful as well.

It is important, however, to point out at once some things the Study Guide cannot do and is not intended to do:

1) It cannot be used instead of the Civilization textbook, since the items indicated in the outline of the Study Guide are neither explained nor interconnected except in the Civilization textbook;

2) It cannot be expected to give all the possible essay questions, especially questions in which the student is asked to evaluate material or present opinions; and

3) It does not provide sample objective questions of either the "True and False" nor the "Multiple Choice" type, but the list of TERMS, PEOPLE, AND EVENTS has been made long enough to provide almost all such items from the Chapter. The student who is careful to be able to recognize each of these items, and is familiar with the places in the MAP EXERCISE, should do well in objective tests. For other students, there may be more items in each of these lists that are necessary, but the Study Guide is designed for all students.

One of the most important features of this Study Guide is the topical charts, most of which have been used for many years. If you will look at the first of these at the end of Chapter 1, you will see that the textbook mentions fourteen areas of civilization and says something about them under twelve possible topic headings. In addition, your instructor probably will supply additional information in lectures and supplementary reading not covered in the textbook. You will note that this first chart contains a total of 168 separate items, represented by boxes, but it is obvious that not all of these will be covered in enough detail to make it possible for you to know more than a few lines about some of them. According to how much extra material your instructor provides, you should be able to know which of the items you could be asked to describe at some length in an essay test.

Items from the chart might be used as part of an essay question in which the   student would be asked to do one of these two things:

       a) Compare and contrast five of the geographic areas of civilization in one of the topics, such as religion; or

       b) Compare and contrast two of the geographic areas of civilization (such as Mesopotamia and Egypt) under five of the topics.

In addition to the endless "compare and contrast" questions which the chart suggests, the student should also be able to describe, discuss, explain, or evaluate many of the single items. Thus, the student who understands the important items and has thought about them may well be able to answer most possible questions. Not every chapter in the textbook can be arranged in such a chart, but useful comparison charts will be given where ever possible.

Another feature of the Study Guide is the chronology charts, which can be used to visualize on a time chart the comparative development of each of the civilizations, or in later sections to compare periods in the development of each country or of various countries in western civilization.

<u>MAP EXERCISE</u>: Map No. 1, Europe and the Near East in 1939

Constant reference is made in the textbook to modern countries, so that the student may visualize the historical
locations in reference to modern times. In order to make
this more meaningful, we should begin with a map of Europe
and the Middle East in about 1939, when there existed more
independent countries than before or since.

<u>Locate</u> and be able to identify:

Albania	Lebanon
Algeria	Libya
Arabia	Lithuania
Austria	Luxembourg
Belgium	Morocco
Bulgaria	Netherlands
Czechoslovakia	Norway
Denmark	Palestine
Egypt	Poland
England	Portugal
Estonia	Rumania
Finland	Russia
France	Saudi Arabia (Arabia)
Germany	Scotland
Great Britain	Spain
Greece	Sweden
Hungary	Switzerland
Iran	Syria
Iraq	Tunisia
Ireland	Turkey
Italy	Wales
Jordan	Yugoslavia
Latvia	

Union of Soviet Socialist Republics

Chapter 1

Man's First Civilizations

In the vast totality of all matter, Man and his world are of minor statistical significance; in the total time span of the existence of matter, the era of Man is but a mere moment; and even in the brief time that Man has existed on this minute planet, the period we really know much about is short indeed. In this first chapter, we shall examine early Man and the history of Man since the discovery of record keeping some 5,000 years ago. Yet, in this one short chapter we must deal with more than half of the record of what Man has done in all his history, we must hurry through a longer period of time than in the other thirty chapters combined.

Why should we attempt such a task? How can we succeed? What can we learn? And -- says some people today -- who cares?

We all know how psychologists ask their patients to think back to their earliest childhood, to try to remember those first days, so that some strange event or thought in the present can be given meaning in the pattern of a whole life. In the same way, our laws and religion and forms of government and methods of artistic expression all have roots in the past. Most important of all, our language -- the very words and phrases we use to express our ideas of today -- is made up of meanings from our past experience. From our long period of past history, we may be able to see things which will give new meaning to today. In this first chapter, we will learn about our birth and first growth. We may, by getting an overview of a vast period of the past, be able to arrive at some tentative, if illusive, generalizations about our common heritage. In so doing, we may also learn something about the techniques used by historians to study change and make comparisons.

Historians are not convinced that we can learn any mystical or even practical lesson from history and they are certainly not agreed that anyone has discovered any such lesson if one exists, but they are sure that the story of the past is both interesting and well worth trying to understand.

I. Before Writing

    A. Ways we know about the past
       1. Written at the time
       2. Books written since the event
          a. Contradictory accounts
          b. But -- what did people think?
       3. Other evidence

    B. Prehistory (Before written sources)
       1. Age of Earth, Man
       2. Methods of dating
       3. Ancestors of true Man (Homo sapiens)
       4. Events in long, slow advance
          a. Tools
          b. Weapons

    C. Paleolithic (Old Stone) Age
       1. Location
       2. Life, food
       3. Cave paintings -- meaning
       4. Religion -- inferred from paintings
       5. Recent theories of Alexander Marshack
          a. Lunar calendar
          b. Illustrated social life
          c. Illustrated religious beliefs

    D. Neolithic (New Stone) Age
       1. Locations -- all in Near East
       2. Major changes in way of life
          a. Domestication of animals
          b. Domestication of plants
          c. Clay vessels -- art -- food storage
       3. Use of pottery for dating, knowledge of age
       4. Some places of settlement -- life there
          a. Jericho -- buildings there
          b. Catal Huyuk -- life, religion
          c. Jarmo, Uruk, others in modern Iran -- life
          d. Tepe Yahya -- art, religion
       5. Climate as factor in early development
       6. Bronze Age developments
          a. Metallurgy
          b. Writing
          c. Urban Life

7. Areas of Bronze Age development
    a. Tigris-Euphrates valley -- Iran
    b. Nile Valley
    c. Indus Valley
    d. China

II. The Valley Peoples and Iran

A. Subarians in Mesopotamia -- little known

B. Sumerians in Bronze Age (3100 BC)
    1. Locations
    2. Clay tablets as evidence
    3. Government
        a. Organization
        b. Functions
    4. Problems of flooding, farming development
    5. Spread -- east and west
        a. Conquest by Sargon of Akkad (2300 BC)
        b. Disunity
        c. Gudea of Lagash unites (2050 BC)
        d. Ur -- rise and decline
    6. Religion
        a. Various gods, meanings of
        b. Beliefs
    7. Family, life, economy, laws
    8. Literature -- story of Gilgamesh
    9. Art, Architecture (ziggurat), statuary

C. Tepe Yahra and Iran (3500 BC)
    1. Recent clay-tablet discoveries
    2. Elamite language
    3. Various areas
    4. Life of times

D. Akkadians: Babylonians and Assyrians
    1. Conquest of Sumeria (2300 BC)
        a. Akkadian language
        b. Life, economy seen from clay tablets.
    2. Hammurabi, code of laws (1700 BC)
        a. Social features -- classes, rights
        b. Economic features
        c. Crime and punishment
    3. Kassite conquest and rule (1530-1130 BC)
    4. Assyrian conquest and rule (1130-612 BC)
        a. Character of Assyrian militarism
        b. Government

5. Mede conquest, from Iran (612 BC)
6. Babylonian revival period (612-538 BC)
   a. Empire extent, influence
   b. Brilliance of period, fame of
   c. Hebrew conquest and captivity
7. Persian conquest by Cyrus the Great ends separate existence (538 BC)
8. Babylonian and Assyrian Religion - Science
   a. Debt to Sumerians
   b. Various gods
   c. View of life, their history
   d. Astronomy, astrology, mathematics
   e. General gloomy tone
   f. Demonology
9. Art and architecture
   a. Debt to Sumerians
   b. Stone buildings
   c. Military sculpture

III. Egypt

A. Generalizations
   1. Influence of geography
   2. Comparison with Mesopotamia in spirit and character
   3. Geographic districts and influences
   4. Government, bureaucracy, priesthood

B. Periods
   1. Old Kingdom (2850-2200 BC)
      a. Kings and religion
      b. Bureaucracy, governors, priesthood
      c. Disunity, decline
   2. Period of disunity (2200-2000 BC)
   3. Middle Kingdom (2100-1800 BC)
      a. Territorial expansion -- Palestine, Syria
      b. Centralization of government
      c. Decline, weakness
   4. Hyksos conquest and foreign rule (1800-1550 BC)
   5. New Kingdom (1550-1085 BC)
      a. Foreign conquest -- Mesopotamia, Nubia
      b. Local and foreign rule
      c. Amenhoteps and religious upheaval
      d. Decline and growing weakness
      e. Invasion of the "Sea People"
   6. Gradual decline, conquest by foreign invaders

C. Religion
   1. Various gods, cults
   2. Cult and story of Osiris, Isis, Set, and Horus
   3. Life after death; the <u>ka</u>

D. Egyptian writing, language

E. Literature
   1. <u>Book of the Dead</u>
   2. Stories and romances (Sinuhe)

F. Art, architecture, sculpture
   1. General features, examples
   2. Realism and reflection of daily life

IV. People Outside the Valleys

A. Background factors in common
   1. From mountains, deserts -- not valleys
   2. Indo-European ethnic origins
   3. Kings head of nobility
   4. Military use of horses, chariots
   5. Divided conquered land equally
   6. All Near Eastern peoples used Akkadian
      (Semitic) language for correspondence

B. Hittites
   1. Sources of our knowledge
   2. Location -- Anatolia (Hattusas -- Bogazkby)
   3. Military-political history
      a. Extent of empire
      b. Influence of Egypt on king-god idea
   4. Religion -- many sources
      a. Unusual role of women
      b. Cremation of kings
   5. Language
   6. Literature (first treaties)
   7. Architecture

C. Hurrians
   1. Location -- Mitanni, Mts. north of Mesopotamia
   2. Hittite influence of religion, society
   3. Important role as intermediaries north and west

D. Canaanites
   1. Location -- Ugarit, coast of Syria
   2. Wide influence -- Greeks, Hebrews

3. Literature
    a. Official business
    b. Epic poetrv -- hero Krat
4. Political, religious localism
    a. Many gods -- overlapping
    b. Human sacrifice, temple prostitution
    c. Baal and Astarte

E. Phoenicians
    1. Location -- northern Syria
    2. Famous for trade, whole Mediterranean
        a. Carthage -- colony in 800 BC.
        b. Language (Punic), alphabet spread
        c. Gods adopted elsewhere -- Greeks

F. Hebrews
    1. Old Testament sources
        a. First history in series of books
        b. Varied subjects, types
        c. Sacred to Jews and Christians
        d. Problem of historical accuracy
    2. Migrations
        a. Begin in Ur (Sumeria)
        b. Left Ur (1950 BC)
        c. To northern mt. area (Harran).
            Early accounts common to area:
            Creation, flood, Eden. Tower of Babel
        d. Western migration (1500 BC)
            Canaan area of northern Syria
            Hittite, Hurrian, Egyptian contacts
            Wanderers, raiders -- captives
        e. Nile Delta -- Kyksos period
        f. Exodus from Egypt (1300 BC)
    3. Political history in Promised Land
        a. Long war with Canaanites, Philistines
        b. Loose confederation, religion common
        c. Monarchy begun under Saul (1020 BC)
            Solomon strengths
            Division into two kingdoms (933 BC)
        d. Conquest by Assyrians, Babylonians
        e. Cyrus (Persian) frees (538 BC)
            Return to Palestine area
            No state of own -- religion holds
                together
            Persian, Macedonian, Roman rule
    4. Religion
        a. Notable features

    b. Holdovers from nomadic period
    c. Fundamental ideas
        monotheism -- no images -- may not use
        name of their god -- historically
        oriented customs
    d. Moral code
    e. Ark of the Covenant
    f. Prophets and the course of history

  5. Social customs, law

V. Crete and Mycenae

  A. Minoan (2600-1300 BC)
    1. Location -- why called Minoan
    2. Sources of our knowledge
        a. Sir Arthur Evans and Palace at Knossus
        b. Linear A Script -- mystery of
    3. General features -- learned from pottery art
        a. Overseas empire
        b. Art & architecture of Palace of Minos
        c. Pottery, painting
        d. Social life
    4. Mystery of sudden fall, burning of Palace

  B. Mycenaea (200-111 BC)
    1. Influences of geography of mainland   Greece
    2. Minoan -- Mycenaean trade and influences
        a. Government and art
        b. Mycenaean record keeping -- Linear B
    3. Politics and society
        a. Not empire builders
        b. Loose confederation on mainland
        c. Tombs, palaces, furniture, vibrant life
    4. Religion

  C. Trojan War (1200-1250 BC)
    1. Iliad as source of our knowledge
    2. Problem of historical accuracy
    3. Mythical and true events

  D. Invasions of the "Sea People"
    1. Who were they? Dorians?
    2. Invade and ruin Egypt, Phoenicia, Crete,
       Anatolia, Greece

E. Dark Ages (1100-800 BC) as result
  1. Literacy, writing, hand skills vanish
  2. Gradual recovery -- use of iron
  3. Odyssey from this period
     a. General story of
     b. How handed down, finally written

TERMS, PEOPLE, EVENTS

Old Stone Age
New Stone Age
Bronze Age
Neolithic
Paleolithic
archeology
mythology

Gilgamesh
Cyrus the Great
Marduk
Code of Hammurabi
Indo-European
Akkadian
Semitic

Rosetta Stone
Book of the Dead
ka
Osiris
Isis
Amenhotep IV (Akhenaten)
Tutankhamen
hieroglyphics
Hyskos invasions

Iliad
Odyssey
Homer
Linear A, Linear B
Palace of Minos
Agamemnon
Troy VI, VII
Ritual bull game

Abraham
Moses
Exodus
David
Saul
Solomon
Ten Commandments
Old Testament
Ark of the Covenant

MAP EXERCISE Map No. 2, The Ancient Near East

Locate these bodies of water:
Black Sea, Caspian Sea, Aral Sea, Aegean Sea, Mediterranean Sea, Dead Sea, Red Sea, Persian Gulf.

Locate these rivers:
Tigris, Euphrates, Indus, Jordan, Nile.

Locate the areas of earliest civilization.

Locate these areas:
Crete, Cyprus, Asia Minor, Anatolia, Syria, Assyria, Media, Phoenicia, Akkad, Sumer, Mesopotamia, Chaldea, Palestine, Israel, Judaea, Philistaea, Upper Egypt, Lower Egypt, center of Hittite civilization, and the center of Hurrian civilization.

Locate these ancient cities:
Mycenaean, Troy, Knossus, Ninevah, Assur, Babylon, Ur, Lagash, Tyre, Jerusalem, Jerico, Rosetta, Memphis, and Thebes.

Locate the modern areas of Greece, Turkey, Iraq, Iran, Jordan, Arabia, and Egypt.

Locate the modern cities of Baghdad, Damascus, and Cairo.

	Before Writing		Mesopotamia			Egypt		
	Paleolithic	Meolithic	Sumerian	Babylonian	Assyrian	Old Kingdom	Middle Kingdom	New Kingdom
Geography and Location								
People, their language								
Economy; homes, food, life								
Social Structure Customs								
Government -- Law								
Religion								
Culture — Painting Sculpture								
Culture — Architecture								
Culture — Literature								
Culture — Science and Technology								
Culture — Philosophy								
Character or Spirit								

Non-valley People					Crete, Aegean		
Hittites	Hurrians	Caanites	Phoenicians	Hebrews	Minoanians	Mycenaeans	Troy

SAMPLE QUESTIONS

See the chart for sample "compare and contrast" questions.

1. Describe and discuss the role of geography on Egypt, Mesopotamia, the Phoenicians, Crete, and Greece.

2. Compare the philosophy of law to the Code of Hammurabi, Egypt, the Old Testament, and Homeric Greece.

3. Compare the influence of religion on Egypt, Mesopotamia, the Hebrews, and the Early Greeks. Account for the importance of religion in this period.

4. Describe the "common" feature of the ancient civilizations in their economy, social structures, governments, way of life, and religion. How do you account for this similarity?

5. Describe and evaluate our "debt" to the Ancient World.

6. What do we mean by the "style and character" of a civilization? Describe the "style and character" of each of the major civilizations.

7. What are the general characteristics of the Hebrew religion? Which of these were retained in Christianity? Which not retained? Which modified?

8. Describe, explain, and account for the many discoveries made in the past twenty-five years about the Ancient World.

Chapter 2

The Greeks

Ancient Greece! No other civilization has had quite the love, admiration, and affection heaped upon it; no other demonstrates just how much we owe to the past; and no other shows how often we are unaware of our debt.

We go through our daily life using Greek words, aiming at Greek ideals, and measuring beauty and harmony in Greek values. We sprinkle our conversation with references to "sour grapes, innocent as a lamb, slow as a tortoise, sly as a fox, a stupid ass," etc., without always knowing that these familiar types come from Aesop's Fables. Most of our political terms and many of our political models come from the Greeks, who invented aristocracy, oligarchy, tyranny, and democracy. Modern psychology uses terms to identify personality traits taken from Greek drama, for Freud selected these terms to order to make identification of the precise characteristics easy, since he knew that all "educated" people had read the famous Greek plays. The very terms "drama" and "tragedy" and "comedy" are Greek words and the types of dramatic situation we call pathos, humor, satire, or burlesque are based on Greek plays. Great stories of the heroes of the past and their thrilling lives come from the models of epic poetry laid down by Homer. Philosophy begins with the Greeks and continues to ask most of the same questions and frames answers in imitation or rejection of Greek methods of logic and classification. History (and Geography) began with Herodotus and Thucydides originated the study of war and politics as the most dramatic and important of all historical events. Science, especially the pure sciences of mathematics and physics, began with the Greeks.

We could go on and on, but this should be enought to begin to understand just how "relevant" Greek civilization is to our own experience.

TOPIC OUTLINE

I. The Greeks before the Persian Wars

    A. The Greek style and character
       1. Curious
       2. Delight in life

    a. Less otherworldly
    b. Human answers to human problems
   3. Invented many forms of government
    a. Democracy, oligarchy, aristocracy,
     tyranny
    b. Practice fell short of ideals
   4. Humor
    a. Drama -- satire; raucous and even cruel
     laughter
    b. Also energetic, inventive, opinionated,
     arrogant, quarrelsome

B. Greek revival after Dark Ages
  1. Renewed contacts with east
    a. Phoenicians through Cyprus
    b. Ionian islands, coast
  2. Orderly life resumed
  3. Influence of the poet Hesiod
    a. Rules for "proper" farmer
    b. Genealogy of the gods
    c. Longing for the "good old days"
    d. Stand for social justice

C. Growth of polis (city state)
  1. Physical plan (acropolis, agora)
  2. Social change with new military role
    a. Rich, nobility dominate politics
    b. Farmers, craftsmen, merchants lose out
  3. Rise of tyrants to solve class conflict

D. Colonization
  1. Causes (overpopulation, class strife)
  2. Areas of colonization, extent
  3. Growing Greek trade domination

E. Sparta
  1. Location -- village system
  2. Classes (Equals, helots, perioikoi)
  3. Lycurgus' Constitution
  4. War training, discipline
  5. Economy -- iron money
  6. Culture -- war poetry

F. Athens
  1. Early government
    a. Aristocratic, tribal
    b. Class basis of power

                    clansmen -- guildsmen
        c. Branches, powers
           general assembly
           Archons -- leaders
           Council of Areopagus
    2. Crisis of power -- class strife
        a. Draco -- 1st code of Athenia law
           famous for harshness
           aristocratic, agricultural
           debt laws -- farmer, artisan slavery
        b. Solon -- legal reform
           equality under law -- debt reform
           dommerce aided -- end agrarian dependence
           Council of Four Hundred
           Economic program makes   Athens rich
        c. Solon resigns, strife returns
           artisans of coast
           farmers of hills   (areas, classes)
           aristocrats of plains
        d. Peisistratus (546-510 B.C.)
           Nobleman -- tyrant
           Political program
           Economic program
           Nobles oppose him -- he favors poor
        e. Cleisthenes (508-
           New tyrant -- favors the guildsmen
           Grants equality in elections
           New demes (1) end hill-plain-coast split
           Council of Five Hundred   created
           organization
           functions
           All citizens now can have political
           experience

II. Persia and the Greeks to 478 B.C.

    A. Sources of our knowledge

    B. Persia -- rise and growth
        1. Mesopotamia conquered by Medes, Persians
        2. Cyrus (550-529 B.C.)
           a. Persians conquer Medes
           b. Expansion -- Hebrews freed
              Syria Anatolia Egypt
              Ionian Greek cities
           c. Political, religious policies

                          -19-

3. Darius (529-486 B.C.)
   a. Zoroastrianism adopted
   b. Empire expanded
      Europe invaded
      Danube basin, Ukraine
   c. Ionian Greeks revolt Athens aids
      Greece invaded
      Marathon defeat
      Athenian prestige high
      Miltiades -- role of
4. Xierxes (486-465 B.C.) plans new invasion

C. Xerxes invasion of Greece
  1. Athens -- rise ostracism -- Themistocles
  2. Greek League formed
    a. Spartan land leadership
      Thermopylae (480) defense
      Athens abandoned
    b. Athenian naval rise
      Salamis victory (480)
      Xerxes withdraws
    c. Persians back, Plataea defeat (479)
    d. Mycale defeat (478) ends danger
  3. Unity from the Leage and wars

III. Athenian Empire
  A. Rise from Delian League
    1. Naval alliance -- against Persia
      Athens dominates -- Spartan opposition
    2. Advantages, disadvantages for allies
  B. Political reform in Athens
    1. Pericles rise -- role of
    2. Areopagus Council (aristocratic) ended
    3. New citizenship New juery system
    4. Democracy, expenses, citizens role increase
    5. Prosperity, public works
  C. Delian League pays the bill
    1. Treasury to Athens
    2. Persia forced out of Ionian cities
    3. Resentment grows -- Aparta feeds on
  D. Peloponnesian War (431-404 B.C.)
    1. Causes -- Sparta fears Athenian growth
      a. Invasion of Attica
      b. Pericles' strategy of defense
      c. Plague
      d. Class strife over peace
    2. Peace under Nicias (421-416)

        3. Alcibiades rise character
            a. Sicily invasion disaster
            b. Hermes statue mutilation question
        4. War resumes (Athens, Sparta, Persia)
            a. Alcibiades switches sides
            b. Athens debates democracy or oligarchy?
            c. Athens defeated, surrenders
            d. Atrocities

IV. The Fourth Century and the Hellenistic Age

    A. Period of Spartan domination (404-368 B.C.)
        1. Instability
            a. Polis against polis in Greece
            b. Class strife in each polis
            c. Persian advances in Ionian cities
        2. Boeotian League -- anti-Sparta -- Thebes heads
            a. Sparta defeated
            b. Power ended

    B. Period of domination by Thebes (368-338 B.C.)
        1. Epaminondas -- democracy spread
        2. New League (362) -- Athens as rival
        3. Prosperity -- capitalism -- trade

    C. Rise of Macedon (359-336 B.C.)
        1. Location, people
        2. Government -- military tactics
        3. Philip as regent (359-336 B.C.)
            a. Victory in north
            b. Defeat of Thebes and Athens
            c. New "Greek" League (337)
            d. Invasion of Asia Minor
            e. Government of new "allies"
            f. Ancient Homeric patriotism restored

    D. Alexander the Great (336-323 B.C.)
        1. Place in history
        2. Course of his conquests
        3. Policies towards conquered areas
            a. Persian marriage, "ways"
            b. Tension with Macedonians
        4. What if he had lived? His significance.

    E. Heirs of Alexander
        1. Division of empire
            a. Ptolemies in Egypt

                    Policies   Greek influences
                    City of Alexandria
               b. Seleucids in Asia
                    Policies
                    Comparisons with Ptolemies
               c. Antigonids in Greece & Macedon
                    Policies -- Antigonas Gonatas
                    Celtic invasion
          2. Growing separation, discord

V. Religion, Writing, and Thought in Greece

     A. Religion
          1. The gods
          2. Cults
               a. Demeter
               b. Dionysus -- leads to drama

     B. Tragedy
          1. Characteristics -- purposes
          2. Aeschylus
               a. The Persians
               b. Prometheus Bound
               c. Oresteia
          3. Sophocles
               a. Antigone
               b. Oedipus at Colonus
          4. Euripides
               a. Hippolytus
               b. Medea
               c. Alcestis
               d. Trojan Women
               e. Bacchae

     C. Comedy
          1. General characteristics -- purposes
          2. Aristophanes
               a. The Frogs
               b. The Clouds
               c. Lysistrata
               d. The Birds
          3. Tne New Comedy -- Menander

     D. Lyric Poetry

E. History
   1. Herodotus -- Persian Wars
      a. History of Persian Wars
      b. Reliability of
   2. Thucydides -- Peloponnesian Wars
      a. Compared with Herodotus
      b. Insights, methods
   3. Xenophon -- follows Thucydides
   4. Arrian -- Alexander's campaigns
   5. Polybius, Greek -- Roman history

F. Science -- theory over practice
   1. General characteristics
   2. Hippocrates and medicine
   3. Pythagoras and mathematics
   4. Democritus and the atom
   5. Alexandria as later center
      a. Astronomy (Aristarchus, Eratosthenes, Hipparchus)
      b. Geometry (Euclid)
      c. Physics (Archimedes)

G. Scholarship
   1. Rhetoric
   2. Sophists
      a. Wisdom men -- wide interests
      b. Question everything
            Why? How? What? Always?
            Are you sure? Really?

H. Philosophy
   1. Socrates -- Sophist, "gadfly"
      a. Socratic method
      b. Theories
      c. Trial and death
      d. Influence of
   2. Plato
      a. Methods
      b. Theory of Ideas -- parable of cave
      c. The Republic -- Philosopher-King
      d. Influence of
   3. Aristotle
      a. Wide interests -- methods
      b. Classification in politics, science
      c. Golden Mean
      d. Influence of
   4. Epicurean and the "golden mean"

5. Stoics (Zeno) repress physical desires

I. General Greek Spirit
   1. Everyday life vs. generalizations
   2. The Greek contribution
       drama -- democracy -- philosophy
       Know Thyself -- golden mean
       balance -- harmony -- the whole man
       Also excesses -- arrogance -- vices

TERMS, PEOPLE, EVENTS

democracy
oligarchy
aristocracy
tyranny
Pericles' Funeral Oration
Hesoid
polis
Lycurgus' Constitution
Archons
Council of Areopagus
Draco
Solon
Peisistratus
Cleisthenes
deme
Council of Five Hundred
Cyrus the Great
Darius
Zoroastrianism
Xerxes
Battle of Marathon
Battle of Thermopylae
Battle of Salamis
Delian League
Pericles
Persian Wars
Peloponnesian War
Alcibiades
Boeotian League
Philip of Macedon

Demeter
Dionysus
Aeschylus
Sophocles
Euripides
Aristophanes
Herodotus
Thucydides
Sophists
gadfly
Socrates
Plato
Aristotle
Epicurean
Stoics
golden mean
Know thyself

MAP EXERCISE: Map No. 3, The Ancient Greek World

Locate these seas:
> Black Sea, Aegean Sea, Ionian Sea, Adriatic
> Sea, Mediterranean Sea

Locate these areas and islands;
> Asia Minor, Pelloponesus, Attica, Euboea, Rhodes,
> Crete, Delos, Laconia, Boeotia, Macedonia, Thrace.

Locate the Bosporus, Hellespont, Propontis.

Locate these cities:
> Troy, Miletus, Knossus, Thebes, Athens, Sparta,
> Corinth, Olympia, Byzantium, Delphi, Piraeus,
> Argos, Mycenae.

Locate these battle sites;
> Thermopolae, Marathon, Salamis.

Show the area of the Athenian Empire in 450 B.C.

MAP EXERCISE: Map No. 4, Alexander's Empire

Locate the Aegean, Black, Caspian, Red, and Mediterranean
    seas and the Persian Gulf.

Locate the Danube, Tigris, Euphrates, Indus, and Nile
    rivers.

Locate the areas of Macedonia, Thrace, Epirus, Greece,
    Ionia, Asia Minor, Armenia, Assyria, Media, Par-
    thia, Bactria, India, Persia, Syria, Egypt, and
    Cyrenacia.

Locate the cities of Pella, Thebes, Athens, Sparta, Byzan-
    tium, Pergamum, Sardis, Antioch, Tyre, Jerusalem,
    Memphis, Alexandria in Egypt, Babylon, Persepolis,
    Ecbatana, and the Oasis of Siwah.

Trace the route of Alexander.

Show the division of Alexander's Empire after his death.

Show the extent of the Persian Empire at its height.

SAMPLE QUESTIONS

1. Describe and discuss the influence of geography on the Greeks.

2. Compare and contrast Athens and Sparta in geography, economy, social structure, government, culture, and spirit.

3. Describe, discuss, and evaluate the Spartan tradition of discipline. What effects did it have?

4. Describe, discuss, and evaluate the Greek polis and show how it was the basis of Greek greatness and of the eventual decline of Greece.

5. The Greeks have given us four types of governmental organization: aristocracy, oligarchy, democracy, and tyranny. Define each carefully and give examples.

6. Describe and discuss the class basic of each of the political terms in question #5. What class conflicts and changes contributed to changes from one to another?

7. What were the strengths and weaknesses of Athenian democracy? Was Athens really democratic?

8. Compare and contrast the philosophies of Socrates, Plato, Aristotle, Epicurius, and the Stoics.

9. Describe, discuss, and evaluate Greek drama (both tragedy and comedy) and give many examples.

10. Describe, discuss, and evaluate Greek religion and its place in their lives.

11. Compare and contrast the Greek Ideal, the reality of Greek life, and the ugly features of their history.

12. Describe and discuss Greek (including Hellenistic) science.

13. Describe and discuss the causes of the Persian Wars. Why were the Greeks able to win? What were the results on all of Greece? Athens? Sparta?

14. Describe and discuss the causes of the Peloponnesian War. Why did Sparta win? What were the results?

15. The term "tyrant" was used by the Greeks to refer to a type of government, not always bad. Cite specific Greek leaders to show both sides of this definition.

16. Account for the fact that intellectuals of the Western Civilization have so admired the Greeks in general and Athens in particular.

17. Explain the many complicated features of the Athenian democracy and show why these large and often clumsy political bodies and agencies were the heart of the system and both its strength and its weakness.

18. Describe and discuss the career of Alexander the Great. Does he really deserve to be called "Great?" Give evidence for and against the use of the appellation.

19. Explain how the Greek world before and After Alexander was changed and how it remained the same.

Chapter 3

The Romans

Just as the western world has always looked to the Greeks for ideals, so we have learned from the Romans how to make practical application of the ideas of the ancient world. The Romans, without much deep philosophical contemplation, had to change their system of government from a rather typical Greek-style oligarchy to a Republic. The Roman Republic was a practical compromise worked out bit by bit to prevent serious class strife from turning into permanent civil war. First the common people and then the new classes were given roles in government. As Rome grew into a mighty Empire, so too the government changed to give some degree of local government and even Roman citizenship to the new peoples. The institutions and administrative techniques of Roman government became models for others. Both the Republic and the Empire eventually failed and we have always studied their failure for some clues about the defects which may ruin a system.

The Roman Empire did not last, but it gave western man the vision that a political unit embracing all people might be able to bring peace more be able to bring peace more permanent than the Pax Romana.

Study of the Empire can also show how a country can drift from local wars into imperialism without consciously meaning to do so, and how social and economic problems develop from the empire which vitally affect the "mother" country. But the Romans contributed more than mere practical application of the ideas of others. The Romans had a spirit of their own, a sense of personal and family and social duty which has inspired many others. They developed practical written laws to fit their needs, but soon found that laws, no matter how carefully framed, cannot bring true justice without a firm application of what the Romans came to call equity, the case-by-case flexibility of the letter of the law to guarantee that the spirit of the law is applied to particular needs.

Their sense of the spirit of the real law also led them to desire to frame human law in such terms as to have it coincide with natural law, knowing that the law cannot endure unless it is in agreement with human nature and human conduct.

-29-

Finally, the Romans gave us their language, Latin. Most of the languages of the western world are taken from the Latin, the real mother tongue of the west. It became the language of the Church, of the law and the courts, of education and scholarship, and eventually of science.

TOPIC OUTLINE

I. Rome of the Republic

A. Background
1. Mythical founding
2. Geography   Italy - Greece compared
3. Etruscan period (700-509 B.C.)
    a, Etruscan characteristics
         language mystery   art
         economy   religion
    b. Expulsion (509 B.C.) Tarquin the Proud
4. City state formed   free -- small

B. Early Republic (509 - 133 B.C.)
1. Class basis of citizenship
    a. Patricians
    b. Plegeians
2. Political organization
    a. Consuls
    b. Dictator -- for emergencies
    c. Senate   S.P.Q.R.
    d. Centurian Assembly
3. How patrician became consul (praetor, censor)
4. War -- the business of the Roman state
    a. Army organization   phalanx, legion
    b. Army membership   discipline
5. Plebeian rise
    a. Objections -- main weapon
    b. Tribunes of own (491 B.C.)
    c. Tribal Assembly to pass on laws (471 B.C.)
    d. Law (written) of Twelve Tablets (451 B.C.)
    e. Economic gains -- debt slavery
        new land   limit on farm size
        farmer-debtor problem remains
    f. Equal rights in politics (366 B.C.)
        hold any office   can intermarry
        <u>nobiles</u> -- new class

C. Roman expansion (509-113 B.C.)
1. Steps in Italy
    a. How Italy was governed
    b. Colonies
    c. New "part" citizenship

2. Punic Wars (265 - 146 B.C.)
   a. Causes first clash with Carthage
   b. First War -- Sicily
   c. Second War
      Hannibal into Italy
      Scipio into Africa
   d. Third War
      Delenda est Carthago (Cato)
      Spain -- "Africa" as provinces
3. Greece, Balkans, Asia Minor
   a. Causes Roman involvement
   b. Macedonian invasion
   c. Asia Minor
   d. Into Greece -- sack of Corinth
   e. Growing Roman prestige

II. Crisis of the Republic (133 - 27 B.C.)

A. Basic causes
  1. Troubles in the new Empire
    a. Government new areas -- citizenship
    b. New rich class --   new wealth flows to
                       Rome
  2. Economic distress in Italy
    a. Decline small farms
    b. Growth latifundia -- new rich -- slavery
    c. New rich from colonies -- growth equites
                        class
    d. landless to Rome
  3. Social, political tensions -- growth factions
    a. optimates -- no change
    b. populares -- equality new classes; new
                citizens

B. Reforms of Tiberius and Gaius Gracchus (133-121)
  1. Political
    a. Tribunal Assembly over Senate
    b. New power to tribunes, equites class
    c. Citizenship expansion
  2. Economic
    a. latifundia limited
    b. Land for the landless -- new colonies
    c. Cheap grain for Rome
  3. Results
    a. Economic, political failure
    b. Violence, civil war, murder
  4. Evaluation Gracchi period

C. Rise of the Generals -- civil war
1. Marius -- champion of populares
   a. Army reorganization   professional soldiers
   b. Citizenship extended
   c. War in Greece   Sack of Greek treasures
2. Sulla -- champion of Senate; optimates
   a. Senate powers back
   b. populares crushed
   c. Greek war continued
3. Pompey
   a. Tribal Assembly, tribunes back to power
   b. Greek war against Mithridates
   c. Syria, Asia Minor new provinces
   d. Gatiline conspiracy -- Cicero rise
4. First triumvirate
   a. Pompey, Crassus, Caesar
      Crassus to Parthia -- killed
      Caesar to Gaul (See Special Section)
      Pompey to Spain
   b. Pompey vs. Caesar
      Pompey back to Rome -- sole consul
      Caesar returns from Gaul
         Campaigns in Spain, Greece, Egypt,
         Asia Minor, North Africa, back to Rome
      Defeat, death of Pompey
5. Dictatorship of Caesar
   a. Subversion Republican institutions
   b. Economic program
   c. Social program
   d. Building "new" Rome
   e. Murder of
   f. Problem evlauation of Caesarism

The Gauls: Special Section

1. Sources knowledge -- Caesar's Commentaries -- others
2. Description
   a. Location -- geography
   b. Social customs, dress, physical appearance
   c. Government -- punishment for crime
   d. Classes (druids, nobles, common people)
   e. Arts and crafts
   f. Religion, magic, druids, sacrifices
3. Influence on Rome -- Influence Rome on Gauls

6. Second Triumvirate
   a. Why formed after murder Caesar
   b. Octavius -- Anthony -- Lepidus
      who they were
      territorial split
      opponents   tactics
   c. Elimination Brutus & Cassius
   d. Death of Lepidus
   e. Anthony & Cleopatra
   f. Triumph of Octavius

III. The Roman Empire (27 B.C. - 180 A.D.)

A. Octavius Augustus (27 B.C. - 14. A.D.)
  1. Objectives -- methods
  2. Program in Rome
    a. Own powers
    b. "Reform" of Senate
    c. Careers open to talent
    d. Army reform   Veterans benefits
    e. New tax system
    f. Social laws
    g. Building program
  3. Foreign affairs
    a. Parthia
    b. Palestine
    c. Spain and Portugal
    d. New possession along northern border
    e. German disaster (9 A.D.)
      Expansions ended
    f. Meaning of the Pax Romana

B. Successors to Octavius Augustus
  1. Four poor emperors (14-68)
    a. Tiberius
    b. Caligula -- terror under
    c. Claudius
      citizenship extended civil service rise
    d. Nero
      personal life -- burning of Rome
      rebellion in the empire
  2. Vespasian, sons (69-96)
    a. Senate -- citizenship
    b. Provinces, rebellion -- army reform
  3. Adoptive system (96-180)
    a. Technique   Senate role
    b. Trajan   Dacia campaign

        c. Hadrian
            Empire: walls, peace, travel
            Economic: prices, taxes, debt
            Legal: law code, slavery, soldiers
            Army changes
        d. Antoninus Pius and Marcus Aurelius
            Peace   prosperity   high culture
            Stoicism   Good government for all
            Growing pressure from Germanic tribes
    4. The Downward Slide (180-284)
        a. Commodus -- tyrant without talent
        b. Septimius Severus, his sons
            civil war again   guard disbanded
            new rights, powers for troops
            citizenship to all in Empire
        c. Period of many emperors (42!)
            Troops pick man   Soon murdered
            military domination
            growing pressure from invaders
            growing weakness   provinces secede
            plague   foreign invasions
            population decline   public order vanishes

C. Revival -- The "new" Empire (284-337)
    1. Diocletian (284-305)
        a. Political program
            Oriental despotism, great pomp
            succession -- tetrarchy system
            Administration decentralization
                Provinces, dioceses, prefectures
            Bureaucracy -- new officials over senators
        b. Economic, social stratification
            taxes to freeze workers to land, jobs
            civitas -- new tax collector class
        c. Bleak period
            corruption, violence, vice, despair
            inequity and inequality of justice
        d. Evaluation -- collapse delayed

D. Problem of decline of Rome
    1. Historical debate
        a. Gibbon -- religion
        b. Rostovtzeff -- class struggle
        c. Racial dilution -- Climate
    2. Economic causes
        a. Population decline   plague, war
        b. latifundia, elimination small farmer

c. Alienation masses from leaders
   3. Barbaric pressure compounds rest

IV. Roman Religion, Writing, and Thought

A. Greek influences
   1. Arts -- entire inspiration
   2. Literature -- Greek techniques, Roman spirit
   3. Science, engineering   Romans more talent -- both
   4. Government and law

B. Religion
   1. Early -- household spirits, spirits of nature
   2. Etruscans -- divination -- predict future
   3. Greeks -- adopted their gods, changed names
   4. Imperial cult
      a. State religion, priests, temples
      b. Masses seldom bothered with it except
         holidays
      c. Lost appeal for all quickly
   5. Eastern mystery cults
   6. Christianity (See later chapter)

C. Literature
   1. Quintus Ennius (from Magna Graecia)
      a. Homer as model -- epic poetry
      b. <u>Annales</u> -- celebrated military virtues
   2. Drama
      a. Menander, New Comedy of Greece, as model
      b. Plantus -- raucous
         stock characters   originality
         used by later dramatists -- Shakespeare
      c. Terence -- closer to Greek models
      d. Village farces -- crude, obscene
   3. Poetry
      a. Lucretius
         Stoic, close follower of Epicurus
         No afterlife   gods do not run us
         Nature -- fixed law -- runs universe
      b. Catullus -- love poetry
   4. Cicero and prose
      a. Oratory -- science and art of
         Senate speeches, letters to friends
         Stoicism explained
         Natural law -- law of nations
         seek harmony in laws

5. The Golden Age -- Octavius Augustus period
   a. Augustus as patron, admirer of arts
   b. Vergil -- poetry
      Aeneid -- birth of Rome -- her future
                               glory
      pastoral poetry -- praise simple, rural
                                 life
      Augustus as patron
   c. Roman character -- quiet toughness
   d. Ovid -- poetry
      Art of Love -- cynical to extreme
      myths
   e. Livy -- history
      History of Rome in 142 volumes
      Roman virtues stressed
6. Silver Age
   a. Tacitus -- history
      Germania -- study of the Germans
      praise of simple, rugged life
      praise of what Rome has lost: character
   b. Seneca
      Stoicism praised, but satire on Claudius
      influence on Claudius
   c. Lucan -- epic poetry
      Epic of civil war, Caesar and Pompey
   d. Persius -- drama
   e. Juvenal -- satire, drama

D. Roman Law
  1. The Twelve Tablets -- written law
  2. Growth of law
    a. jus gentium -- law of the peoples
    b. Equity
       spirit, not letter, of the law
       judges must be aware of
       precedent
    c. Natural Law
       highest law -- above man's laws
       make man's laws conform with
    d. Heritage of Roman law
       basis of most modern law
       spirit of the laws

E. Medicine
  1. Surgery advanced -- Caesarean operation
  2. Hospitals -- civilian -- military
  3. Galen (a Greek) main contributor

F. Ptolemy, of Alexandria, and Geography

V. The Legacy of Rome Evaluated

A. The Empire -- peace and prosperity for 200 years
   1. High standard of living
   2. Slums, poverty, bread and circuses
   3. Brutality, gladiators, public executions

B. Influence on the West
   1. Easy to see
   2. Long lasting

TERMS, PEOPLE, EVENTS

Etruscans
Tarquin the Proud
patricians
plebeians
consul
dictator
Senate
Centurian Assembly
tribunes
Twelve Tablets
nobiles
Punic Wars
Hannibal
Scipio Africanus
latifundia
equites
optimates
populares
Gracchi reforms
Tribal Assembly
Marius
Sulla
First Triumvirate
Pompey
Julius Caesar
Second Triumvirate

Lucretius
Cicero
Golden Age
Silver Age
Vergil
Horace
Ovid
Livy
Tacitus
jus gentium
natural law
equity
Galen
Roman citizenship
Caesarism
tetrarchy
Marcus Aurelius
Stoicism
druids
Diocletian
Octavius Augustus
Mark Anthony
Cleopatra
Pax Romana
Hadrian
Adoptive System

<u>MAP EXERCISE</u> Map No. 5, The Roman World

<u>Locate</u> the Mediterranean Sea, Adriatic Sea, Atlantic
      Ocean, North Sea, Black Sea, Red Sea.

<u>Locate</u> the Danube River, Tiber River, Rhone River, Rhine,
      Po rivers,

<u>Locate</u> the cities of Rome, Alexandria, Carthage, New Car-
      thage, Massilia, Cannae, Messana, Syracus, Byzantium,
      Antioch, Jerusalem, and Memphis.

<u>Locate</u> the areas of Hispania (Spain), Gallia (France),
      Britannia, Illyricum, Macedonia, Thrace, Palestine,
      Egypt, Cyrenaica, Numidia, Mauretania, Epirus, and
      Dacia.

<u>Locate</u> the island of Malta.

<u>Locate</u> the line of division of the Roman Empire into East
      and West.

<u>Locate</u> the Rhine-Danube Wall, Hadrian's Wall, and the Wall
      of Antoninus.

<u>Show</u> the development of the Roman Empire in these periods:
  a) Rome, the city-state
  b) At the start of the 1st Punic War (264 B.C.)
  c) At the end of the 3rd Punic War (146 B.C.)
  d) At the death of Caesar (44 B.C.)
  e) At the death of Augustus (14 A.D.)
  f) At its greatest extent

SAMPLE QUESTIONS

1. Describe the major features and accomplishments of Roman Law.

2. Discuss the historical debate over the causes of the decline of the Roman Empire.

3. Later ages called Augustus the founder of the Roman Empire, but he called himself "the restorer of the Roman Republic." Cite evidence to support both sides of this statement. Which do you believe to be correct? Why?

4. Show how the expansion of Rome into Italy and then into the Empire increased and intensified existing problems and conflicts in Rome; how it added new ones.

5. Describe the class basis of the early government of the city-state of Rome. Describe and discuss the institutions of this early government.

6. Describe and discuss the growth of economic problems for the plebeians during the expansion of Rome into Italy.

7. Describe and discuss the causes, stages and events, and results of the Punic Wars.

8. Describe the geography, social organization, social customs, government, arts, and religion of the Gauls. Why did Tacitus admire them? What was their influence?

9. Describe the main items in the program of Julius Caesar in the government, army, tax system, social problems, building program, and the Empire.

10. Evaluate the contributions of Augustus to the Pax Romana.

11. What were the chief political, economic, and social problems which caused the Gracchi brothers to make major changes in the Republic? What was their program? Why did it fail?

12. Explain how the failure of the Gracchi reforms led to the chaos of the period of the struggle of the various generals for power.

13. Trace the changes in the government of Rome through these periods and stages:
    (a) Early Roman government about 509 B.C.
    (b) Liberalization from 449 B.C. to 133 B.C.
    (c) The Gracchi reforms 133 - 112 B.C.
    (d) Marius and Sulla 112 - 80 B.C.
    (e) Julius Caesar and Caesarism
    (f) Augustus

14. Describe and discuss the Greek influence on Roman culture.

15. Describe, discuss, and evaluate Roman literature, including epics, drama, poetry, history, and prose.

16. Compare and contrast the literature of the Golden Age and of the Silver Age.

17. How did Rome expand from a small city-state into a giant empire? To what extent was this expansion -- often called imperialism -- an accident and to what extent was it deliberate? Explain.

18. How was the Roman Empire governed? Describe and discuss the central administration, the local administration, the place of local home rule in the empire, the problem of citizenship, and the factors which led to holding the empire together.

19. Describe and discuss changing attitudes and cults in Roman religion.

20. Describe, discuss, and evaluate the Roman ideas of a good Roman.

The Art of Greece and Rome

The Art of Greece and Rome

C. The "Classical" Age (450 - 400 B.C.)
  1. Architecture -- Acropolis
     a. Parthenon
     b. Propylaea
     c. Temple of Athena
     d. Erechtheum
  2. Sculpture
     a. Phidias' style dominates -- Parthenon
     b. Counterpoise technique
     c. "severe" style replaces "archaic style"
     d. Bronze castings
  3. Painting
     a. Large examples lost -- names, descriptions
     b. Vases
        red-figured technique for common use
        lekythois -- fancy oil jug -- tomb use

D. "Post Classical" Age (400 - 30 B.C.) Hellenistic
  1. Architecture
     a. Corinthian column -- offshoot of Ionic style
     b. Town planning -- town squares
     c. Outdoor theatre
     d. Mausoleum, a tomb, example all future types
  2. Sculpture
     a. Praxiteles -- examples lost   copies
        copies: Hermes -- Aphrodite
     b. Apollo Belvedere
     c. The dying Gaul -- also only copy remains
     d. Winged victory of Samothrace
        greatest Hellenistic masterpiece
     e. Many small works -- for private sale
     f. Coins
  3. Painting, floor-mosaics
     a. Everyday life
     b. Passions of "common" men

III. Etruscan Art
   A. General Characteristic follow Greek period
   B. Vase painting
   C. Bronze work most famous
      1. Statutes, mirrors
      2. Famous she-wolf   religious?
   D. Architecture -- true arch

IV. Roman Art
   A. Main trends and periods
      1. Early period
         a. Romans busy with war, politics, money
         b. Etruscans supply art
      2. Hellenistic period
         a. Booty from Greece (painting, statues)
         b. Gato opposition
         c. Increased flow   Greek artists to Rome
         d. Revival of serene style of Phidias
      3. Imperial period
         a. Spread through empire, Atlantic to Near East
         b. Not finale of Greek art, decayed
         c. Roman style; own elements, innovations

   B. Architecture
      1. General characteristics
         a. New materials   concrete
         b. New use of old techniques   barrel-vaulting
         c. Use of all three Greek "orders" at once
      2. Types, examples
         a. Temple   maison caree
         b. Aqueducts
         c. Theatre, amphitheatre -- Colosseum
         d. Public Baths
         e. Town hall (basilica) -- Constantine's
         f. Private houses (villa)
         g. Circular temple --Pantheon

   C. Sculpture
      1. General features
         a. Greek classical techniques
         b. Roman character -- gravity, calm
      2. Types, with examples
         a. Large plaques   Altar of Peace
         b. Portrait sculpture
            death mask -- exact copy of wax mask
            bust only -- Augustus
            Many still exist -- all sorts of people
         c. Triumphal arch -- Arch of Titus
         d. Sculptured frieze
            series of pictures, winds up column
            Columns of Trajan, Marcus Aurelius

   D. Painting
      1. Types, with examples
         a. Floor mosaics   at Pompeii

   b. Wall painting Pompeii -- Livia's garden
  2. Themes
   a. Historical epics -- religious epics
   b. Whole cities with building, people, harbor
   c. Details of daily life -- myths

 V. General evaluation (Art of Greece and Rome)
  A. Variations in time and place
  B. Unique, unified in totality
  C. Unique when compared with earlier centuries
  D. Sharp change after period
   1. Christianity -- new needs, outlook
   2. Barbarian invaders -- also new outlook

TERMS, PEOPLE, EVENTS

Geometric Age
Archaic Age
red-figure style
kylix
The "archaic smile"
Greek architectural "orders"
Doric
Ionic
Corinthian
Classical Age of Art
Parthenon
Phidias
counterpoise
"severe" style
lekythois
Praxiteles
floor mosaics
amphitheatre
Colosseum
maison carree of Nimes
basilica
villa
Pantheon
Death mask
Triumphal arch
Pompeii

1. Compare and contrast the (a) pottery, (b) sculpture,
   (c) painting, and (d) architecture of Greece in these
   periods:
   > Geometric Age
   > Archaic Age
   > Classical Age
   > Post-Classical Age

2. Describe and discuss the (a) pottery, (b) sculpture,
   (c) painting, and (d) architecture of the Etruscans.

3. Compare and contrast the (a) pottery, (b) sculpture,
   (c) painting, and (d) architecture of the Romans in
   these periods:

   > Early Rome
   > Hellenistic Age
   > Imperial Age

4. Compare and contrast Greek and Roman art in general
   under these headings:
   > (a) pottery
   > (b) sculpture
   > (c) painting
   > (d) architecture

5. Discuss the idea that the art of Greece and Rome are
   essentially one evolutionary development, not two
   separate developments. Cite specific evidence both
   for and against the idea that they are products of
   only one development.

Chapter 4

Christianity

This chapter has the potential of being especially difficult for students. In the first place, one of the main aims of the chapter is to put the life of Jesus and the struggles of early Christianity in their historical setting, yet some students may be upset by any such attempt and most have never considered the undoubted fact that Jesus was born into a real world full of real problems. Indeed, the message and claims of the early Christians will be shown to have been part of important disputes in Palestine. The persecution of the Christians, the non-religious reasons for these persecutions, the political im-plications of the growth of Christianity, the competition with Christianity from other religions which had something to offer, will all be discussed. For those who have always viewed these things only as religious, and especially for those who have assumed that the victory of Christianity was the only possible result, this may be disturbing and will certainly be a new approach.

Secondly, some students may read the chapter with less concentration than usual out of the impression that they know the material and have been exposed to it for years. Since the chapter takes an historical view, such an assumption will almost surely be an error.

Thirdly, students may be upset by the section on the basic ideas and practices of Christianity. I myself dis-agree with some of the statements and I would be surprised if all students do not find at least one item they ques-tion. Careful reading will show that the authors say that there is disagreement over these ideas, and, after all, a large section is an account of the heresies which arose from the very beginning. If this chapter gives you a deeper understanding of Christianity, one of the things you should learn is that the probability of dispute is one of the basic symptoms of the vitality of Christianity. All religions give answers to most of the same questions, but the fact that the answers in Christianity are not clear cut and often raises new questions. So, our disagreement is part of the very strength and essential character of Christianity.

Finally, students should note the connection between

Christianity and other religions and civilizations in addition to the obvious connection with the Hebrews.

TOPIC OUTLINE

I. Religion in the Later Roman World
   A. Romans, religion, and science
      1. Industrial revolution near
         a. Greek science, Roman technical skipps
         b. Steam engine discovered
      2. Romans scorned research, feared invention
         a. Spirit against science
         b. Unemployment danger

   B. Romans look at the future
      1. Pessimism replaces reasional progress ideal
      2. Man cannot work out future
      d. Gods no help either
         a. Fortune -- cult of goddess of
         b. Fate -- future fixed
         c. Cicero, Vergil, Tacitus attitudes

   C. Astrology
      1. Astronomy gives way to astrology
         a. Seven planets -- 7 days -- 7 magic number
         b. Twelve houses of Sun
      2. Emperiors, people turn to astrology
      3. Magic

   D. New Cults
      1. State religion loses appeal -- for masses
      2. General features new cults
         a. Save soul
         b. Myth or story of saviour -- person
         c. Purification by ritual
         d. Guarantee of afterlife
      3. Dionysus, called Bacchus
         a. Celebrate animal side of man
         b. Rites -- drink, sex
      4. Cybele
         a. Story of
         b. rites
         c. temples
      5. Isis -- feminine following
         a. Story of
         b. rites

6. Mithra -- men, soldiers especially
   a. Initiation by trial
   b. rites -- temples
   c. self-denial

E. Philosophy and Mysticism
   1. Intellectuals, upper clas
   2. Epicurianism
      a. Ideas on fear, the gods, life, afterlife, evil
      b. Followers
      c. Why not widely followed
   3. Stoicism
      a. Ideas on human nature and emotions
      b. How to live, face evil, see universe
      c. Why not successful
   4. Hermes
      a. Ideas
      b. Followers
   5. Neoplatonism
      a. Philosophical ideas
      b. How to live
      c. rites

F. Christianity
   1. No cult (above) wide appeal -- reasons
   2. Competition between cults
   3. Christianity too -- for 300 years

II. Jesus and the First Christians
A. Historical problem: birth, life, death

B. Jewish society of time
   1. Political and historical development
      a. Seleucid rule -- Hellenization of Jews
         class split, strife
      b. Maccabean rebellion -- Hasmoneans, Assidaeans
      c. Roman intervention -- Pompey -- Caesar
      d. Reign of Herod (37-4 B.C.) -- program of
         Hellenization again -- Jewish response
   2. Three parties in Roman period
      a. Sadducees -- aristocrats
         Political, religious ideas
      b. Pharisees -- branch of Assidaeans
         Political, religious ideas

c. Essenes
        Source -- Dead Sea Scrolls
        monastic community -- cities too
        rituals -- religious ideas
        reformers -- much in common with
                Christians
    d. Zealots -- Israel: the true Jews
        Came after Jesus   anti-Roman
        Political ideas, practices
3. Roman treatment of Jews
    a. Most privileged subjects
        political rights
        religious rights
        Anti-Jewish feelings by others in Empire
    b. Jewish view of Romans
4. Conclusion: Jesus born into troubled,
    divided land

C. Teachings of Jesus
    1. Social message
        a. Attitude towards "Good" life
        b. Treatment of others
        c. Human nature
    2. Theological conclusions
        a. The Messiah -- meaning
        b. Result of acceptance, rejection his
            teachings
        c. Baptism -- Last Supper
    3. Response of Jewish authorities
    4. Crucifixion -- Resurection
        a. Meaning
        b. Promise of future history
        c. Second Coming
    5. Parallel, unusual teachings
        a. Some Judaism -- other cults
        b. Crucifixion as sacrifice
        c. Promise of reward for followers
        d. Appeal in immediacy, in no others

D   D. The First Christians
    1. Who were they
        a. Earliest followers
        b. Wide appeal of the "glad-tidings"
        c. Paul and the gentiles
        d. Dispute over Jewish Law
    2. Epistles, Gospels
        a. When, how written
        b. Other books

3. The Judaeo-Christians
   a. Who they were
   b. Teachings, practices
   c. Why this died -- Why gentile church won
4. Paul and his influence
   a. His travels
   b. Message to the gentiles
   c. Greek influences upon him, teachings
      This world vs. next world
      Real vs. Ideal
   d. Paul and church discipline
5. Christians in Roman Empire
   a. Paul, Peter in Rome
   b. Peter -- traditions about
   c. Attitudes in Rome towards Christians
   d. Extent, location, size new sect
   e. Conclusions

III. Christianity in the Pagan World

A. Reasons for persecution
   1. General Roman policy: toleration
   2. Roman officials and the Christians
   3. Public opinion on
   4. Christians and the state religion
      a. compared with other sects
      b. Public disobedience

B. Nature of persecutions
   1. Sporadic
   2. Nero (Tacitus on)
   3. Pliny the Younger -- Trajan answer
   4. Punishment "for the name alone" -- why
      a. Contrasted with treatment of Jews
      b. Blamed for all disasters
      c. Public opinion

C. Persecution to domination
   1. Persecution at its height (249-311)
      a. causes
      b. Decius -- official day of state ceremony
      c. Valerian
   2. Conversion of Constantine
      a. Story of
      b. results
   3. Theodosius -- Christianity as official
      religion

a. Persecution of pagans begins
b. Christian attitude on toleration changes

D. Why did Christianity triumph?
1. Beginning not promising
   a. Despised sect
   b. Rich, sophisticated society
2. Advantages over mystery cults
   a. Religion of love in savage period
   b. Jesus' teachings (which see)
   c. Missionary priesthood
   d. Appeal to both sexes
   e. Ritual dramatic, beautiful
   f. Exciting, dangerous to be part of
3. Ideas, rites from other sects
   a. Makes conversion easier
   b. Acceptance of ideas of others
4. Conclusions
   a. New mixed with old -- message of Love
      New promise -- preserve familiar
   b. Church organization also important

IV. Organization of the Church

A. Why organization needed

B. Early organization development
1. Bishop (episkopos) over see
   a. Headquarters in Roman civitas
   b. Doctrine of Apostolic Succession
2. Archbishop (archiepiskopos) over province
   a. Group of sees, bishops
   b. Headquarters in metropolis, mother city
3. Pope (papa) in Rome, imperial city
   a. Why Roman leadership
      Prestige of Rome   Peter and Paul
      Petrine Theory
   b. Rival claims for leadership
   c. Growth papal political power

C. Characteristics of Church government in west
1. Change in response to need
2. Use of existing machinery, capitals
3. Council of bishops and archbishops
   a. Approve or reject ideas, practices
   b. Selected 27 books of New Testament
      Greek, Latin (Vulgate) Bible
      Other books, rejected, still survive

-53-

D. Local organization
  1. Bishop has several churches
     a. Church area (parish) has priest, deacon
     b. Early -- Elders (presbyteries) select
        officers
     c. Later -- appointment from above
     d. Laity -- clergy -- distinction grows
  2. Hierarchial organization
     a. Changing powers, relations between elements
     b. Councils vs. popes -- dist serious issue
  3. Church and State
     a. State officials, public interest, influence
        Appointment of bishops, others
        Church role in politics
     b. Pope wants ultimate power
     c. Dispute into eleventh century over issue
     d. Difference -- East -- West
        East -- power rests in State
        West -- long struggle over

E. Monasticism
  1. Secular clergy -- serves laity
  2. Regular clergy -- life by rule
     a. Early monks -- practices -- ideals
     b. Growing need for rules
     c. St. Basil and Greek monasteries
        Celibacy, poverty -- reject world
        hard work - charity - hospitals -
        orphanages
     d. St. Benedict and Latin monasteries
        Hard work -- missionaries to pagans
        Aid to poor, sick
        Monastic scholar, scribe -- importance of
        Self-supporting community
  3. Secular vs. Regular clergy
     a. Which more important?
     b. Bishop or abbot as regulator
     c. Reform of monasteries, convents

V. Ideas of Christianity

   A. Role of Clergy

   B. Salvation
      1. Baptism and Original Sin
      2. Eucharist and link with God
      3. Meaning of life and death of Jesus

4. Goal of immortal happiness
5. Disputes over meanings
   a. Relationship of Father and Son
   b. Meaning of Original Sin
   c. Role of Church and clergy
   d. Faith or good works?

C. The Seven Sacraments
   1. In Roman Catholicism
      a. Baptism
      b. Confirmation
      c. Eucharist (Communion, Lord's Supper)
      d. Penance
      e. Extreme Unction (Last rites)
      f. Ordination
      g. Matrimony
   2. Protestants
      a. Baptism, Communion accepted by most
      b. Penance most vigorously rejected

D. Heresy
   1. Meaning of term -- importance
   2. Gnostics, Manichaenists
      a. Problem of evil in world created by God
      b. Dualism (Parallel in Zoroastrianism)
   3. Donatists
      a. Historical problem
      b. Ideas of
      c. Constantine "solution"
   4. Arianism
      a. Central idea -- Father and Son
      b. Why important
      c. Athanasius' answer
      d. Council of Nicaea -- Nicaean Creed
      e. Constantine and Caesaropapism
      f. Continuation of heresy -- spread
   5. Nestorians, Monophysites
      a. Problem of the two natures of Christ
      b. Ideas of each
      c. Council of Chalcedon (451)
      d. Continuation of heresy -- East, West split

VI. Thought and Letters in the First Christian Centuries

A. East - West split increases
   1. Causes
   2. Results

B. Pagan literature declines
   1. Emperor Julius (361-363)
   2. Christian attitude towards pagal classics
      a. Greeks and classical education
         Basil, Gregory of Nyassa,
         Gregory of Nazianzos
      b. Classical scholars in the West
         Jerome and the Vulgate translation
         Ambrose views Cicero

C. Augustine (354-430)
   1. Early life
      a. North Africa in his day
      b. Education, family life
      c. Manichaeanism adopted
      d. Ambrose, Stoicism, Neoplatanism
      e. Conversion and baptism
      f. The Confessions -- story of his spiritual
         journey
   2. Augustine as Bishop of Hippo
      a. Donastics -- persecution of
      b. City of God
         Explains fall of Rome
         Christianity not cause
         Real causes explained
      c. Pelagius and Julius of Eclanum
         Ideas of -- influence
         Augustine answer -- persecution of
         Original Sin and Free Will
   3. Old Age -- Predestination doctrine

V. The Christian Way of Life

   A. Relationship with God

   B. Distrust of senses, rationalism, human per-
      fectability

   C. Individualism and unselfishness

   D. Society -- Love, charity, forgiveness

   E. Striving for good, a better world, helping others

   F. Universality of appeal

TERMS, PEOPLE, EVENTS

Fortune
Fate Dionysus
Cybele
Isis
Mithra
Epicurianism
Stoicism
Hermes
Neoplatonism
Maccabean Revolt
Herod
Saducees
Pharisees
Zealots
Essenes
Dead Sea Scrolls
The Messiah
The Judaeo-Christians
Paul
Peter
Pliny the Younger
Emperor Decius
Bishop
see
Archbishop
province
Pope
Petrine Theory
Vulgate Bible
hierarchial
Secular clergy
Regular clergy
Apostolic Succession
St. Basil
St. Benedict
Original Sin
Eucharist
Penance
Sacraments

Gnostics
Manichaean
Dualism
Arianism
Council of Nicaea
Nicaean Creed
Caesaropapism
Nestorians
Monophysites
Council of Chalcedon
Heresy
Ambrose
Augustine
Confessions
City of God
Predestination
Pelagius
Donastics

SAMPLE QUESTIONS

1. Describe and discuss the life of Jesus in its historical setting under these headings:
   a) General political situation
   b) Jewish sects and divisions,
   c) The Romans and the Jews,
   d) Probably response to teachings of Jesus

2. Describe, discuss, and evaluate the general religious
atmosphre in the Roman Empire af the time. Describe
the various cults, their strengths and weaknesses, and
the attractions of each.

3. Describe, discuss, and evaluate the life, writings, and
influence of Augustine.

4. Define "heresy" and explain the general problem. Describe, discuss, and evaluate the six early heresies
and their impact.

5. Account for the gradual supremacy of the Bishop of Rome
in the West and explain why he did not gain the same
position in the East.

6. Trace the spread of monasticism and compare and contrast Eastern and Western monasticism.

7. Describe and discuss the organization and administration of the early Christian church. Explain the issues
which came to produce conflict between church officials
and/or groups and between church and state.

8. Account for the development of the difference between
the secular clergy and the regular clergy and explain
the conflicts which developed between the two.

9. Describe, discuss, and evalutae the contributions of
St. Paul to Christianity.

10. What problems developed for the followers of Jesus im-
mediately after his death? What were the possible al-
ternatives? What groups and issues developed? Why did
the position of St. Paul triumph?

11. Explain the importance of Baptism and the Eucharist in
early Christianity to overcome Original Sin and gain
Salvation.

PERIOD ROUNDUP

The Ancient World

	Paleolithic Neolithic	Mesopotamia	Egypt	Non-Valley People	Hebrews	Myceneans Minoians	Athens	Sparta	Roman Republic	Roman Empire	Gauls	Etruscans
Geography												
People, their Language												
Economic												
Social												
Government and Law												
Religion												
Culture — Painting												
Culture — Sculpture												
Culture — Architecture												
Culture — Drama												
Culture — Poetry												
Culture — History												
Culture — Science												
Culture — Technology												
Culture — Philosophy												
Character and Spirit												

SAMPLE QUESTIONS

1. (From the chart)
   Describe, discuss, and evaluate the influence of
   geography upon Prehistory, Egypt, Mesopotamia, the
   Hebrews, Greece, Alexander's Empire, Rome, the Roman
   Republic, the Roman Empire, and the Gauls.

2. Do the same for economics.

3. Do the same for Social Structure; for Government; Law;
   Religion.

4. Compare and contrast the Character and Spirit of
   Egypt, Mesopotamia, Athens, Sparta, the Hellenistic
   Empire, the Romans, the Gauls, and the Hebrews.

5. Compare and contrast the culture of the Greeks and the
   Romans.

6. Compare and contrast the general cutlural achievements
   (with specific examples) of Egypt, Mesopotamia, Sparta,
   Athens, the Etruscans, and the Romans.

7. Describe and discuss the idea that Greek, Hellenistic,
   and Roman civilization are not separate, but an evolutionary continuation of one basic civilization.

8. Account for the fact that the Greeks and the Romans
   did not take religion as "seriously" as did the other
   civilizations of the ancient world.

9. We tend to use the terms "democracy" and "republic" to
   mean the same thing. Explain the difference in the
   terms with specific reference to Greece and Rome.
   Show how and why each developed and what things in
   each civilization produced that type of governmental
   organization.

10. Most of the civilizations of the ancient world had
    social systems which were very similar. Explain the
    basic pattern of social organization, show where there
    were differences and account for these differences, and
    account for the basic similarity in all the civiliza-
    tions.

MAP EXERCISE Map No. 6, The Ancient World

With various colored lines, show the extent of these
large empires:
    The Assyrian Empire to 625 B.C.
    The Persian Empire to 500 B.C.
    Alexander's Empire to 325 B.C.
    The Roman Empire to 117 A.D.

Identiy these important bodies of water:
    Atlantic Ocean, Black Sea, Caspian Sea, Mediterranean
    Sea, Aegean Sea, and the Red Sea

Locate these important rivers:
    The Tigris, Euphrates, Nile, Danube, and
    Rhine

Locate these important cities:
    Baghdad, Ur, Jerusalem, Damascus, Jerusalem, Memphis,
    Thebes, Alexandria, Troy, Constantinople, Athens,
    Corinth, Sparta, Antioch, Rome, Carthage, Knossos,
    and Mycenae.

Locate these important areas:
    Egypt, Mesopotamia, Syria, Palestine, Asia Minor,
    Greece, Macedonia, Italy, Gaul, Spain, Sicily, and
    Crete.

Chapter 5

The West: Early Middle Ages

Between the fourth and the eleventh centuries A.D.,
the Roman emperors, now in their new capital at Constantinople, witnessed the loss of large sections of their Empire
both in the West and in the East. First to be lost was
western Europe, including Britain and the western part of
North Africa, overrun by German invaders in the late fourth
and fifth centuries. Here in western Europe a Roman administration, already in decline, was replaced by an un-
stable group of German kingdoms. Then in the seventh century Arab invaders conquered the populous Roman provinces
in the East, leaving to the Byzantine Empire, as this late
Roman Empire is called, only the Balkan peninsula and Asia
Minor.

The present chapter begins the story of the Germanic
peoples in the West and carries their history up to the
eleventh century. This period is called the Early Middle
Ages, or Dark Ages, and is the first of two periods into
which the history of the Middle Ages is commonly divided.
The events of the late Middle Ages, from the eleventh
through the fifteenth centuries, will be the subject of
three later chapters.

The history of western Europe in the Early Middle Ages
is essentially an account of what happened to Roman civilization, already weakened by internal decline, when it
was struck from without by a series of barbarian invaders,
first German and later Norse and Magyar. Under such conditions Roman economy, political structure, culture, and
religion understandably suffered and deteriorated. Only
the ideal of One World lived on; for awhile it existed in
fact in the organization of the Church and in Charlemagne's
attempts to revive the Empire in the West. But in the
ninth and tenth centuries even these vestiges of centralized authority in Church and State collapsed and were replaced by local, autonomous units of feudalism. Earlier,
the even more localized and self-sufficient agricultural
economy of the manor had replaced the industry, commerce,
and money economy of Rome. An accompanying decline in
thought, art, and religion completed the disintegration of
Roman civilization.

In this chapter, we should concentrate on the symptoms

of the collapse of Roman institutions, the results of the various invasions, the rise and decline of Charlemagne's Empire, the development of the political power of the Papacy, and the development of the two most lasting institutions of the early Middle Ages; the manor and feudalism.

TOPIC OUTLINE

I. Breakdown Roman Civilization (500-1000 A.D.)

  A. Problem of terms
    1. Dark Ages?
      a. Real decline -- Compare with Classical ages
      b. Causes external force? Or internal
      c. Familiar historical pattern?
    2. Early Middle Ages?
      a. Improvements, inventions, developments
      b. Things preserved from Classical ages

  B. Germanic invaders
    1. Original locations -- languages
    2. Methods
      a. Types of peaceful infiltration
      b. Types of military intervention
    3. Sources our knowledge
    4. Problem of total numbers; distribution, ratios

  C. Roman breakdown--how complete?
    1. Economic
      a. Communications
      b. Growth local self-sufficiency
    2. Political decline
      a. Empire & local administration; organization
      b. Discipline, morale, law and order
      c. Spreading local wars
    3. Church -- Remaining organization, administration
    4. Culture
      a. Science
      b. Scholarship, original thinking
      c. Decline pure Latin -- rise of vernaculars

  D. What survived?
    1. Simple, every-day tasks
    2. Roman Law -- Roman political ideals
    3. Classical literature -- monestaries -- libraries
    4. Idea of the Empire, Pax Romana as result

E. Groups of invading Germans
  1. General (for each group, below)
     a. Original location
     b. Reasons for leaving -- Problem of Huns
     c. Paths of invasion, migration
     d. Leaders -- contacts with Romans
     e. Final location, kingdoms, modern countries
        from
     f. Influences
     g. Religion (Arian, mostly -- so, heretics)
  2. Groups
     a. Visigoths
     b. Vandals
     c. Angles, Saxons, Jutes
           Celts to Ireland, Scotland, Wales
           Celtic Christianity -
           Irish monestaries, missionaries
     d. Ostrogoths
     e. Franks, Burgundians (See later section)
  3. Asiatic invaders (groups, influences)
     a. Huns
     b. Avars
     c. Bulgars
     d. Magyars (Hungarians)

II. The Franks: Building of an Empire

  A. General Features
     1. Original location
     2. Expansion -- ultimate limits

  B. Merovingians
     1. Clovis as founder
        a. Orthodox Christian -- results
        b. Power, influence
     2. Successors -- inheritance rule of Franks
        a. General results
        b. Fredegund the Wicked as example
        c. Weakness, chaos

  C. Carolingians
     1. Charles Martel
        a. Hereditary family holding of title of Mayor
           of the Palace
        b. Muslims, Battle of Tours
     2. Pepin the Short, his son
        a. Italy -- background

Lombards -- Byzantium -- Papcy
Disunity, chaos, many sides
      b. Pepin and Gregory I agreement
         Pepin as King of Franks
         Invasion of Italy, Lombards defeated
         Donation of Pepin
         Papacy now territorial power
         Forgery of "Donation of Constantine"
   3. Charlemagne, son of Pepin
      a. Einhard, biographer, on his characteristics
      b. Military Exploits -- Extent of his Empire
      c. Government of Empire -- personal nature of
      d. Law and courts
      e. Cultural contributions
      f. Debate over historical importance
   4. Successors
      a. Division of Empire
      b. Growing disunity, weakness
      c. Development of provinces, new areas

III. After Charlemagne

   A. Northmen -- General Characteristics
      1. Scandanavia as base
      2. Causes, methods of raids
      3. Administrative system

   B. Areas of invasion by Northmen
      1. Normandy (In modern northwest France)
         a. Base for new raids
            Mediterranean; Baltic to Russia (Kiev)
            England conquered in 1066
            Ireland (Civilization, monestaries ruined)
         b. Norman administration
      2. Danes vs. Anglo-Saxons in England
         a. Alfred the Great stops -- grants northeast
         b. Canute -- king of Norway, Denmark --
            invasions by
            Made king of England
            Roman christianity adopted, Scandanavia
               adopts
         c. Anglo-Saxon monarchy
            King dominates church and state
            Income, taxes -- Crime, courts, law
            Council (witenagemot)to advise king
            Comparison with Carolingian monarchy

C. Germany (Carolingian decline, rise of Saxon Monarchy
   1. Causes Carolingian decline
      a. Invasions -- Magyars significance
      b. Rise powerful local nobility
         Franconia, Saxony, Swabia, Bavaria
         Duke of Saxony elected as new king
   2. Reign, significance of Otto I (936-973) of Saxony
      a. Dukes, Magyars checked
      b. Italy "invaded"
         Aid Pope against Magyars, Muslims
         Pope crowns him Holy Roman Emperor
         Otto gets right to approve papal elections
   3. Domination of Italy, Papacy by Otto's successors

D. France and Carolingian decline
   1. Growth of power of local nobility
   2. Hugh Capet made king by these nobles
      a. Heirs rule France to 1830
      b. King now less powerful than many nobles

E. Conclusion: Europe about 1000 A.D.
   1. Western Europe
   2. Eastern Europe -- The Eastern Empire
      a. Gradual domination of Slavs; Christianized
      b. Growth difference between East and West

IV. Feudalism

   A. Definition of terms
      1. Who was involved
      2. Reasons for development
      3. Why not a "system"

   B. Historical background -- Origins
      1. German war-band (Gefolge, comitatus)
         a. Chief (Hlaford) and his followers
         b. Method of private army, booty distribution
      2. Roman landlord (patron) and his soldiers (clients)
         a. Landlord and private army
         b. Land grant (fief) in return for military service
         c. Powerful local military men into system
         d. Land (fief) is immune from empire taxes,laws
         e. Titles, grants, etc. become hereditary

-66-

Duke, count, fief, vassal, lord
rights and duties also hereditary

C. Vassals and lords
   1. Feudal practices not uniform
   2. General concepts did exist
      a. Lord (suzerain) owes to vassal:
         fief -- protection -- justice
      b. Vassal owes to lord:
         homage -- fealty -- consel -- hospitality
         feudal aid (military service)
         money gifts on special occasions
      c. Special practices
         investiture -- relief (for heir) -- ward-
           ship
         forfeiture, judgement of peers -- escheat
      d. Feudal chain of command
         king and feudal kingdom
         tenants-in-chief -- rear vassals
         subinfudation -- liege lord
      e. Special complicated practices (examples)

D. Manorialism
   1. On 10% of people involved directly in feudalism
      a. Knights, nobility, families, etc.
      b. Rest -- lives and work on manors
   2. Roman latifundia became manor
      a. Coloni become serfs
      b. Self-sufficient economic unit
         2 field system; 3 fields; fallow
         serf and his strips   lord's demesne
         horse and oxen
      c. Special serf duties
         heriot -- merchet -- use mill, bakery
         roads, ditches, church, priest's land
      d. Church, priests and the serfs
   3. Role of custom
      a. Serf not a slave   Serf-land tied together
      b. Lord's court -- custom prevents exploitation
   4. Manor seldom self-sufficient
      a. Some items absent, shortage, surplus
      b. So, trade desirable and necessary

V. Civilization of the Early Middle Ages in the West

A. General View
   1. Compared with rest of world

Causes, symptoms of low level of culture
a. Who can judge?
b. Period is mixture of classical, new ideas

B. Latin literature -- Italy
1. Boethius (480-524)
a. Translations; including Plato, Aristotle
b. Reconcile Christianity and Aristotle
c. Consolation of Philosophy
    How written   subject matter
    influence at time   later
2. Cassiodorus (490-580)
a. Translates Greek classics into Latin
b. Monastic order -- for copying manuscripts
c. Reconcile classics with Old Testament
3. Pope Gregory the Great (540-604)
a. Practical -- administrative skills
b. Letters to churchmen, churches
c. Writes lives of saints, church fathers
d. Discourages study of classics -- reasons for

C. Latin Literature in Gaul and Spain
1. General
a. Roman purity lessens with distance
b. Gaul an exception
2. Sidonius Appolinaris (231-475) best example
a. Well born, educated. Bishop, country estate
b. Letters -- His life goes on -- no fear, chaos
c. Barbarian invaders, temporary
3. Gregory of Tours
a. Prose chronicle -- Latin is poor
b. But vigour, primitive, honest
4. Einhard, biographer of Charlemagne
a. Also life
5. Theodulf, bishop of Orleans
a. Also life of Charlemagne
b. Both wrote much, traveled, were craftsmen
6. Isidore (570-636), archbishop of Seville
a. Tell of constant invasions
b. Writes Etymologies, an encyclopaedia
c. Great learning; but also superstition

D. Latin Literature in Britain
1. Combination of Roman and Celtic Christianity
a. Great vigor, strength, originality
b. Best of dreary period (700-800)
2. Bede (672-735), an abbot, best
a. Pure and vigorous classical Latin

-68-

      b. History of Church, contact with pagans
      c. Conversion of Anglo-Saxons, their kings
  3. Alciun of York (735-804), student of Bede
      a. Goes to court of Charlemagne
      b. Changes school, leader of Carolingian
         renaissance
      c. Wrote prose, verse

E. Vernacular Literature
  1. Greatest in England
      a. Combination language of Angles, Saxons, Jutes
      b. Translations into Old English -- original
         work
  2. Beowulf, in Old English, greatest
      a. Dispute over author(s), date, place of
         writing
      b. Story of Battles, dragons, voyages
      c. Most remarkable book of whole age

TERMS, PEOPLE, EVENTS

Manor
lord of the manor
serf
demesne
glebe
steward
heriot
mercheat
2,3 field system
fallow
Feudalism
lord
patron
vassal
client
fealty
homage
feudal aids
hospitality
counsel
fief
investiture
primogeniture
wardship
entail
forfeiture
judgement of his peers
escheat
suzerain
tenants-in-chief
rear vassals

subinfudation
liege lord
allod
franklin
Alaric
Theodoric
Attila
Pope Leo the Great
Odovacar
Mayor of the palace
Clovis
Charles Martel
Pepin the Short
Donation of Pepin
Donation of Constantine
Charlemagne
Einhard
Strasbourgh Oath
Alfred the Great
Canute
Otto I (the Great)
Hugh Capet
Carolingian Renaissance
Boethius
Pope Gregory the Great
Sidonius Appolinaris
Gregory of Tours
Bede
Beowulf

1. Why is it important to use the term "Dark Ages" with great caution? Cite evidence both for and against the validity of the term.

2. Define "feudalism: and explain the general practices of feudalism, with emphasis upon the rights and duties of both lord and vassal. (Be prepared to use the terms from the chapter listed in "Terms, People, Places, Events."

3. Why is feudalism not properly called a "system"?

4. Draw a map of a "typical" manor and label   all the parts.

5. Explain in detail how a manor operated, including the daily life of the serfs.

6. Compare and contrast the "idea" of feudalism with the actual "practice".

7. Describe and discuss the sources of the main concepts of feudalism.

8. Describe, discuss, and evaluate the role of custom in both feudalism and the manor.

9. Describe, discuss and evaluate the gains and losses in strength of the Church in the Early Middle Ages. Explain how the Church was able to maintain an effective organization in such chaotic times.

10. Comment on the statement that Charlemagne's Empire was mostly "show and empty titles."

11. Describe and discuss the connection between feudalism and manorialism.

12. Describe and discuss the political and administrative ideas and practices of the Carolingian, Anglo-Saxon, and German (Saxon) monarchies.

13. Describe, discuss, and evaluate the impact of the Huns, Franks, Northmen, Magyars, and Lombards.

MAP EXERCISE: Map No. 7, The West in the Early Middle Ages

Trace the migrations of the Goths, Huns, Vandals, Angles,
    Saxons, Jutes, and Northmen.

Show the changes in these empires:
    Byzantine Empire in 300, 600, 800, and 1000.
    Moslem holdings in 700, 900, and 1000.
    Charlemagne's Empire about 800 and 888.
    Holy Roman Empire and the German Empire in 1000.

Locate the battles of Adrianople, Tours, Troyes, and
    Roncesvalles.

Locate the Avars, Bulgars, Magyars, Lombards, and Slavs.

Identify the important seas and rivers.

Show the holdings of the Anglo-Saxons, the Celts, and the
    Danes after the Peace of Westmore in 878.

Show the Donation of Pepin and the States of the Church
    in 768.

Locate the important medieval cities of Scone, York,
    London, Paris, Aires, Barcelona, Leon, Cordova,
    Pavia, Rome, Naples, Venice, Aix-la-Chappelle,
    Gnesen, Kiev, and Esztergo, Benevento, and
    Constantinople.

Chapter 6

Eastern Christianity and Islam

to the Late Eleventh Century

The question of what happened to the rest of the Roman Empire after the Germans occupied the West and began the formation of a new Western Europe can be answered simply-- it continued. Indeed, it continued for a very long time, over a thousand years, until 1453. The drastic reforms of Diocletian and Constantine in the late third and early fourth centuries seem to have come too late to reverse the decline of the western half of the Empire, but they undoubtedly did much to strengthen and preserve the eastern half. These authoritarian state controls over all aspects of life, particularly evident in the economy and in religion, continued to be characteristic of this later Roman Empire in the East. Here, Roman Civilization did not decline as it did in the West, but it did undergo great modification. It became more Greek, more Oriental, more Christian, and the resulting amalgamation of several heritages is characterized by the name of its capital and greatest city, "Byzantium."

The importance of Byzantium's role as a preserver and disseminator of Civilization, as a buffer protecting the West from eastern invaders, and as the source of much of what is the special character of Eastern European Civilization, has not always received due attention in older textbooks. This was undoubtedly caused by the feeling that it was the civilization of the West, coming to us especially from Britain, that should concern modern Americans. But many of us have a heritage from Eastern Europe as well. Hence the text devotes more space to this story than has been common in the past. This chapter carries Byzantine history -- and the history of the East and South Slavs -- to the end of the eleventh century, covering the period of Byzantium's greatest strength and glory. Much of the history of East Europe is unintelligible without an understanding of Byzantine history.

The chapter also considers the first five hundred years of Moslem civilization. The origins of Islam, the life of Mohammed, and the conditions of the Arabian peninsula did not see auspicious signs for the development of a world movement. Yet in little more than a century,

Islam swept through North Africa and the Near East, pene-
trated Europe and took Spain, and became a dynamic movement
with a unique and important civilization which, while it
borrowed from its neighbors, made new and important contributions of its own. With the modern world having more and
more contacts, it is vital for us to understand some of the
background of a civilization which has been the most dynamic
feature of the life of North Africa, the Near East, the
Middle East, and of Southeastern Asia.

I. Byzantium: The State

    A. Background
       1. Geography of the city, area
       2. Peoples

    B. The Emperor
       1. Political position -- Roman heritage
       2. Religious connection
          a. How chosen -- religious philosophy
          b. How chosen in fact
             Role of senate, army, people
             Adoptive system; violence in process
       3. Political powers
          a. Limitation by "divine law"
          b. Revolutions
          c. Imperial etiquette

    C. Byzantine (Roman) Law
       1. Justinian's Code
          a. How codified
          b. Other laws (Digests -- Institutes -- Novels)
          c. Historical additions (Ekloga -- Basilics)
       2. Justice
          a. Judges, courts, decisions
          b. Role of Emperor

    D. War -- 1100 Years
       1. Areas of pressure
          a. Arabs
          b. Asian (Huns, Avars, Bulgars, Magyars)
          c. European (Slavs, Bulgarians, Russians)
       2. Byzantium as buffern for western Europe
       3. Why original success?
          a. Army: methods, organization, leadership
          b. Navy: methods, Greek fire
       4. Decline of navy -- causes -- results

    E. Diplomacy
       1. Why successful -- methods --philosophy
       2. Use of internal spies; marriage; adoption

F. Economy
  1. Trade (Items, sources, areas)
  2. Monopoly of silk, gold, dye, embroidery
  3. Evidences of graat wealth -- results
  4. Sources of state income
     a. Monopolies -- royal lands -- war booty
     b. Taxation (Results tie of land and labor)

G. The Capital City -- Factions there
  1. Administration of Constantinople
  2. Blues vs. Greens
     a. Chariot-races -- obvious purpose
     b. Political, religious, economic uses
     c. Military, municipal duties
     d. Class, social divisions and rivalry
     e. Riots, violence from system
           Role of Emperor
           Nika Revolt of 532

II. Byzantium and the West

  A. Dominant role of religion in Byzantium
    1. Family life, daily customs
    2. Intellectual influences
    3. Politics and religion mixed
    4. Foreign relation, diplomacy, and war
       a. Church-State unity -- Caesaropapism
       b. Influence on law and clergy
       c. Heresy, Church Councils, and the Emperor

  B. Monasticism; Sacraments
    1. Eastern, western monasticism compared
    2. Meaning, influence of monasticism in East
    3. Ritual, mysticism in Eastern sacraments
    4. Importance of orthodoxy

  C. Schism with West
    1. Problems of image worship; iconoclasm
    2. Papacy under attack
       a. Weak and corrupt popes in 10th century
       b. Balkans, S. Italy removed from Papal power
       c. Papacy rec overs, Normans aid in S. Italy
    3. "Discovery" of word filioque in Roman Creed
       a. Too much like Arianism for East
       b. Cardinal sent to Eastern Patriarch
       c. They excommunicate each other
       d. Formal Schism results -- Lasts to 1965

D. Growing East-West Antagonism
   1. Causes -- distrust, suspicion
   2. Examples from visits, writings

III. Fortunes of Empire (330-1081)

   A. Constantine to Leo III (330-717)
      1. Theodosius and birth of Orthodox Church
      2. Wars, territorial changes
         a. Justinian retakes Roman Mediterranean lands
         b. Syria, Holy Land, Egypt -- lost, retaken
         c. Arabs retak again, North Africa
         d. Lombards threaten all Italy, take north

      3. Administrative reorganization of empire
         a. Division into themes (military districts)
               Military-civil commander combined
               local military-farmer class set up
         b. Emperor keeps imperial units
               Civil service
               Imperial army, own troops
         c. Growth honorary & real hierarchy
      4. Tax reform, changes

   B. Leo III to Basil I (717-867)
      1. Wars, territorial changes
         a. Asia Minor as center of war with Islam
         b. Sicily, Corsica lost to Arabs -- piracy from
         c. Lombards take N. Italy -- Papal States begun
         d. Venice semi-independent
         e. Bulgars begin threat to Balkans
      2. Religious controversy, compromise
         a. Monestaries vs. iconoclastic Emperors
         b. Public opinion pressure, compromise
      3. Free peasantry losing out to large landholders

   C. Basil I to the "Time of Troubles" (867-1081)
      1. Wars, territorial changes
         a. Crete, Antioch, Syria retaken
         b. Armenia annexed -- future troubles from
         c. Italy secured
      2. The Emperor, the "powerful", and the "poor"
         a. Who they are -- Causes, issues between
         b. Basil II and the problem
         c. Results of victory of the "powerful"
      3. Growing weakness, pressures on the Empire
         a. Arabs in Asia Minor

                    b. Normans in Italy
                    c. Bulgars, Magyars, Turks in the Balkans

IV. Byzantine Learning and Literature

        A. General evaluation
            1. Former low opinion in West -- causes
            2. Impartial comparison with West of time

        B. Preservation of Greek Classics
            1. Compared with West
                a. Role of monks in both
                b. Role of prominent men, libraries, teachers,
                    universities in East only
                c. Universities -- Athens -- Constantinople
            2. Our debt to Byzantium

        C. Original writing
            1. Epic story of Basil
            2. History
                a. Popular chronicles, story of Man
                b. Pure history -- with strong bias
            3. Theology
                a. Intellectual, political, popular basis
                b. Controversy over Trinity
                c. Monastic rules; philosophy of monasticism
                d. Platonic mysticism
            4. Popular religious literature
                a. Hymns (role of common people)
                b. Lives of the saints
                    Good source of knowledge about period
                    Christianization of Buddha (Barlaam)

V. Byzantium and the Slavs

        A. Byzantium as transmitter of culture to Slavs
            1. Compare with influence of Rome on Germans
            2. Results on East (On East-West understanding)

        B. The Bulgarians and the Moravians
            1. Location, nationality, culture
            2. Fears of each (Culture, religion)
                a. Bulgarians and Byzantium (Greek Orthodox)
                b. Moravians and Germans (Roman Catholicism)
            3. How they tried to stop "local" influences
            4. Why this failed -- results

C. Byzantine conquest of the Bulgarians
   1. Nature of the war -- results
   2. Bulgarians Greek Orthodox, self-autonomy
   3. Price of Byzantine victory

D. Serbs and Greek Orthodoxy

E. Russia
   1. Early period
      a. Geography and its influences
      b. Scandinavian invasions
      c. Novtorod in north under Rurik
      d. Kiev in Ukraine (south)
           Slavs, Magyars conquered
           Trade with Byzantium
   2. Conversion of the Russians
      a. Early sporadic conversions
      b. Vladimir (of Kiev) conversion (980's)
           Epic story of his conversion
           Reality: many cultural influences
           Forced conversion of Kiev by him
           Marriage alliance seals
      c. Cultural loss as result?
           Greek not forced on Russians
           Local autonomy, appointments, language
           Classics not learned
           But -- purity as results?
      d. Other results
           Rise monasteries, church as landowner
           Trade with Byzantium increased
      e. Paganism remains in rural areas
   3. Kiev Russia
      a. Similarity with Western Europe
      b. Frontier conditions law, society
      c. Trade   (items, directions)
      d. Growing political weakness
           Problem of royal succession, chaos
           Fragmentation into provinces
           Polovtsy invasions -- join factions
   4. Tartar invasion (See next section)

VI. Islam before the Crusades

A. Background
   1. Meaning of terms Islam and Moslem
   2. Historical geographic extent

-79-

B. Life and message of Mohammed
    1. Arabia of the time
        a. Society and politics
        b. Religion -- Mecca and the Kaaba
    2. Early life
        a. Childhood, travels, marriage
        b. Religious revelations
        c. Composition of the Koran
    3. Basic religious ideas
        a. Monotheism -- defined
        b. Afterlife
        c. Duties
        d. Regulation of daily social life
    4. After first revelations
        a. The Hegira, its causes and results
        b. Idea of the jihad, meaning
        c. Return to Mecca -- causes and results
        d. Death -- Extent of Islam at time

C. Expansion of Islam
    1. Causes? Historical debate over.
    2. Early expansion -- areas of
        a. Near East
        b. Mediterranean islands
        c. North Africa and Spain (Battle of Tours,732)
        d. Middle East to Indus River, China border
        e. Africa north of equator
    3. Disunity develops
        a. Unity always lacking in conquered areas
        b. Dispute over succession -- Factions -- wars
        c. Development of sects, separate political units

D. Islamic Civilization
    1. Background
        a. Eastern Roman, Persian areas conquered
        b. Arab religion, language added
        c. Duty of Mecca pilgrimage creates mobility
    2. Arab language -- Study, poetry, influences
    3. Contacts and cultural interchange
        a. Greek, Roman, Persian influences
        b. Byzantium most important
    4. Science
        a. Translation of Greek scientific classics
        b. Mathematics (Indian numerals, zero, algebra,
            geometry, analytical geometry)
        c. Medicine
        d. Physics

5. Philosophy
    a. Greek classics studied, translated
    b. Classics preserved, modified for future
    c. Philosophy, religion, theology
    d. Averroes, Spanish Moslem, most famous
6. Literature
    a. Love poetry -- Arab language role
    b. Adventure -- Arabian Knights -- many sources
    c. Autobiography, history
7. Architecture
8. Music and the dance
    a. Musical instruments, terms from Arabs
    b. Love songs, with dancing

TERMS, PEOPLE, EVENTS

Byzantium
Justinian's Code
Greek fire
Blues and Greens
Nika Revolt of 532
Caesaropapism
Theodosius
Iconoclasm
filioque controversy
themes
The "powerful" and the "poor"
Byzantine monasticism
Byzantine sacraments
Basil II and agrarian reform
Schism of 1054
Novgorod Russia
Kiev Russia
Vladimir's conversion
Polovtsy
Tartars
Islam
Moslem
Koran
Hegira
Battle of Tours
Averroes
Arabian Knights
Ali
caliph
Shiites
Umayyads

SAMPLE QUESTIONS

1. Describe and discuss the role of the emperor in the government of Byzantium. To what extent did the success of Byzantium depend on good emperors?

2. Describe and discuss the factors in the struggle between the Blues and the Greens. To what extent was the later dispute between the "powerful" and the "poor" just a continuation of this basic problem?

3. It is said of Byzantium that "religion pervaded all life." Evaluate this statements.

4. Describe and discuss the causes and results of the great East-West Schism. Discuss the nonreligious factors.

5. Describe, discuss, and evaluate the impact of Byzantium on the Slavs (including the Russians).

6. What differences between Eastern and Western Christianity in theology, ritual, the sacraments, monasticism, images, and leadership made them different?

7. Describe and discuss the respect of Mohammed for Jewish and Christian scriptures and the results.

8. Was the unity of the Moslem world more apparent than real? Describe and discuss this statement.

9. Describe, discuss, and evaluate the factors (religious and otherwise) which led to disunity in Islam.

10. Was the spread of Islam achieved as a holy war, or were there other important factors?

11. Did Byzantium really stop the spread of Islam to Western Europe? Would it have been the great disaster for

civilization which has often been pictured if Europe
had become completely Moslem?

12. What is the "old" view of both Byzantine and Islamic
     culture? To what extent were they imitators only? To
     what extent did they preserve and transmit the classical
     heritage? Modify it? Describe, discuss, and evaluate
     their original contributions in culture.

13. Describe and discuss the main ideas and practices of
     Islam.

MAP EXERCISE: Map No. 8, Byzantium

Locate these bodies of water:
  Mediterranean Sea, Adriatic S h, Aegean Sea,
  Black Sea, Red Sea, Bosporus, Sea of Marmora.

Locate the Danube River.

Locate the islands of Cyprus, Rhodes, Crete, Malta,
  Sicily, Sardinia, Corsica, Balearic Islands.

Locate the areas of the Crimea, Dardanelles, Calabria,
  Apulia, Anatolia, Bithynia, Armenia, Georgia, Syria,
  Egypt.

Locate the cities of Byzantium, Ravenna, Bari, Durazzo,
  Thessalonica, Varna, Chalcedon, Brusa, Nicea, Naples,
  Ephesus, Acre, Tyre, Beirut, Edessa.

Locate the homelands of the Avars, Slavs, Sassanids, and
  Bulgarians.

Locate the line of the East-West religious Schism.

Locate the furtherest extent of the Byzantine Empire;
  the territories lost by 1100.

MAP EXERCISE: Map No. 9, The Spread of Islam

Locate the Atlantic Ocean; the Adriatic, Black, Caspian
       Aral, Red, Arabian, and Mediterranean seas; the
       Persian Gulf.

Locate the areas of France, Spain, Morocco, Libya, Egypt,
       Corsica, Sardinia, Sicily, Malta, Crete, Cyprus,
       Hungary, Transylvania, Moldavia, Wallachia, Serbia,
       Bulgaria, Macedonia, Greece, Anatolia, Syria, Arabis,
       Mesopotamia, Armenia, Persia, Afghanistan, India,
       and the Crimea.

Locate the cities of Algeria, Tripoli, Cairo, Khartoum,
       Tours, Narbonne, Cordova, Granada, Alexandria,
       Vienna, Buda, Pest, Constantinople, Antioch,
       Damascus, Jerusalem, Medina, Mecca, Mosul, Baghdad,
       Kabul.

Trace with a dotted line the route of the Hegira.

Show the spread of Islam by 732 (death of Mohammed), by 656,
       and by 750.

Show the furtherest extent of the spread of Islam, which
       includes the Ottoman Empire.

Chapter 7

Medieval Western Society: The Church and the Empire

This Chapter might be cited as an example of the need to study the total history of a country or a people before making sweeping generalizations about them. Preconceptions about "all Germans" or "all Italians" (See the beginning of the next chapter in the textbook for citation of such hasty conclusions) are superficial at best. Set up as scientific models based on historical evidence ("History proves that...."), they are stereotypes which can lead to dangerous conclusions and catastrophic actions.

This chapter shows the "How and Why" of the evolution of Germany and Italy between 911 and 1273 which formed some of their essential character for the next six hundred years. Both lost political unity and disintegrated into many independent units. Germany retired into particularism, keeping only the fiction of the name as an empire. Northern Italy came under the domination of proud and independent cities, central Italy under the papacy, and Southern Italy and Sicily under various foreign rulers. A long struggle between the papacy and the German emperors, centering around interesting and powerful persons, with both theoretical and practical issues at stake, was to lead to these results. The chapter may also serve to show that the one thing which History may indeed "prove" is that important developments in the history of nations and peoples happen in spite of the fact that few involved foresaw or wanted or tried to achieve any such consequence.

We shall also examine two other important developments in the period: the revival of towns and trade, and the early attempts at reform of the Church, particularly by the new orders of Friars.

Finally, we shall note the role of the Church and the clergy in the genesis of education, particularly the new universities, and the trends in thought which we call Scholasticism.

TOPIC OUTLINE

I. The Society and its Economy

A. Background
1. Eleventh century as turning point
a. Decline Norse raids
b. Offensive against Islam
c. Individual security increased
d. Population growth
Causes -- land clearing -- technology

B. Trade and Towns
1. Causes trade revival
2. Revival towns, new towns
3. Town inhabitants
4. Charters, privileges
a. How obtained
b. Rights granted
5. New industry
6. Craft guilds rise
7. a. Economic functions
b. Non-economic functions
7. Regulation of economy
a. Regulation of competition
b. Economic ideals -- just price -- usury

C. Town and countryside
1. Effect towns on manor
2. a. Marketplace for surplus
b. Refuge from serfdom
2. Growth cash economy
a. Causes
b. Conversion of serf's obligations
c. Results -- role of inflation

D. Fairs
1. Causes, types, locations
2. Functions -- laws of, courts for
3. Bills of exchange

E. Conclusions
1. Society remains mostly rural
2. Rulers, nobility, clergy -- rural outlook of

II. The Medieval Church

A. Background
   1. Who were Church members -- Place of Jews
   2. Church as a super-state
   3. Church - State rivalry as key to era

B. Secular rulers vs. Church and papacy
   1. Attempt of papal absolutism -- Papal weapons
   2. Religious character of feudal monarchy
      a. Religious justification of monarchy
      b. Church sanctions, participation
      c. Religion in coronation, oaths, relics, symbols
   3. Growing secular powers of monarchy -- Church also
      a. Spiritual aura passes to clergy alone
      b. Use clergy by state -- reasons -- results
      c. New monasteries, more monks increase power
      d. Canon law, theological system aid power
      e. Church organization better, more independent
   4. Tradition of Church and Papal powers
      a. Quotes from Christ, Paul, Augustine
      b. St. Ambrose and emperor Theodosius I
      c. Pope Gelasius (492-6) to Byzantine emperor
         Sacred "authority" and royal "power"
         Meaning this? Debate over
   5. Rise, decline of Papal powers in early period
      a. Rise under Pepin, Charlemagne
      b. Tenth century decline
         Immorality of popes -- simony
         Popes dominated by rival Rome factions
      c. Reform under Cluniac movement
         Prestige of Rome (pilgrimage) continues
         Papal duties carried out, even with weak pope
         Mid-eleventh century for real reform

III. Germany and the Papacy, 911-1152

A. Background
   1. Growth 5 powerful duchies, dukes in Germany
   2. King loses control of court, church appointments
   3. Henry I (Saxony) regains powers for king

B. Saxon administration and the Church
   1. Important role of churchmen in government

a. Why kings use them
b. Why church, churchmen willing
c. Good results for both
2. Joint role in Christianization of Slavs

C. The Empire
1. Background
a. East -- Empire as successor to Rome
b. West -- different concept
Claims of German king (as emperor)
Why he would want title, role
2. Otto III and Saxon domination
a. Restoration palace, titles, appointments
b. New heavy German role in Italy
c. Benefits to Germany, Italy, papacy
d. Growth sense of national unity (teutonici)
3. Salian period
a. Saxon line ended, Conrad II (Franconia) in
b. New powers for local minor nobility (counts)
c. Policy fails -- causes -- remedy
d. New ministeriales (administrators) class
Who there were -- non hereditary
Good, unusual results -- nobility response
e. Unusual features in Germany
Efficient administration
Feudalism weak -- Dukes no feudal position
Free men hold free land (allod) New class
Monasteries and tie to free landholder
class
New monasteries and papal ties
f. Failure of revolts

D. The Investiture Controversy
1. Henry III of Germany
a. Deposes 3 popes, appoints own
b. Leo IX (uncle) appointed, begins reform
Monasteries; hierarchy; secular influences
Cardinals; College of Cardinals and elections
2. Gregory VII (Hildebrand) as pope
a. Career, personality, ideas on papal authority
b. Forbids lay investiture (1075)
c. Struggle with emperor -- role of German
nobility
Henry IV "goes to Canossa" (1077)
Traditional, real meaning
3. Civil war in Germany (1077-1122)

a. Causes -- role of pope, nobles, emperor
b. Henry Iv, the Normans, and Gregory
c. Continuation of struggle by successors
   (1085-1122)
4. Concordate of Worms (1122) and lay investiture
   a. Terms on bishops, clerical elections
   b. Terms in Germany -- Burgundy -- Italy
5. Results of civil war
   a. Feudalism, serfdom, particularism in Germany
   b. Norman, commune power grows in Italy
   c. Emperor weakened
   d. Guelf - Ghibeline feud begins

IV. Papacy and Empire: 1152-1273

A. Development legalistic battle
   1. Roman law or cannon law
   2. The Italian Question

B. Frederick Barbarossa (1152-1190)
   1. Empire policies
      a. Clain as successor to Charlemagne
      b. Land consolidation; administration; royal
         power
   2. Italian policies
      a. Roman commune, the pope; coronation (1143)
      b. Diet of Roncaglia and the regalia question
      c. Settlement with the pope)1168)
      d. Peace of Constance, Lombard League, and
         regalia
   3. German policies
      a. Welf lands seized; more feudalism
      b. Powers, rights granted to princes
   4. Marriage policy -- Hohenstaufen and Norman union

C. Henry VI (1190-1197)
   1. Heir to Norman rights in southern Italy
      a. Norman, Moslem, Byzantine policies
      b. Norman government, administration
      c. Holdings, powers expanded in Italy
      d. Mediterranean ambitions -- foreign relations
   2. Feudal rights extended in Germany

D. Pope Innocent III (1198-1216)
   1. General background
      a. His place, importance
      b. Controversy over ideas of papal power
   2. Struggle with Frederick II

                a. Causes; Role of pope, English, French in
                   election
                b. How Frederick won; result
            3. Lateran Council of 1215
                a. Reforms, new rules, new definitions
                b. Crusades, holy war

    E. Frederick II
        1. Why fame as "most interesting" monarch of era
        2. Italian policies
        3. German policies
            a. Grants to princes -- disunity result
            b. Towns, serfs and his policies -- Clergy
        4. Struggle with papacy (1220-12-50)
            a. Lombardy, other issues
            b. Frederick on church corruption; his cures
        5. Papacy and his descendants
            a. End of Hohenstaufen dynasty
            b. Interregnum (1254-1272) and the princes
            c. Princes as real rulers of Germany

V. The Church in Society: Reform and Renewal

    A. Need for reform -- with example
    B. Benedictine monastic reform
        1. Cluny
            a. Aims -- early success -- strengths
            b. Change -- weaknesses
        2. Augustinians
            a. Founding -- aims -- special methods
            b. Good works -- results -- impact
        3. Cistercians
            a. Founding -- aims -- methods -- rules
            b. Success and spread -- conversi role
            c. Economic rules -- results -- feelings against
            d. St. Bernard

    C. The Friars: Dominicans and Franciscans
        1. Urban need for -- The "Apostles"
        2. Founding, early days of orders
            a. Dominicans -- preaching in towns
            b. Franciscans -- example of absolute poverty
            c. How and why both made changes
        3. Later developments
            a. Universities and scholarship
            b. Building -- alms, begging, forgiveness
            c. Reputation for greed -- how attached
            d. Role in Inquisition

D. Education -- Church alone directs
   1. Chaplains and training of upper class youth
   2. Monastic schools -- Training of clergy
      a. Curriculum -- Music, trivium, quadrivium
      b. Preservation of knowledge -- conservative
   3. Cathedral schools
      a. Inquiring spirit -- pagan & classic works
      b. Famous schools -- growth to universities
   4. Universities
      a. Bologna -- students & teachers organize
      b. Paris, others -- college system
      c. "Town and gown" friction
      d. Methods of study, learning

E. Question of Universals
   1. Gerbert of Aurillac (later Pope Sylvester II)
      a. Boethius and Aristotle studied
      b. Logic -- tool for discussion
      c. Explain Bible, church fathers, theology
   2. Problem: universals? (Mankind, dogdom, table-
         dom?)
      a. Nominalists say "no" -- Realists say "yes"
      b. Application -- Individuals and/or the state
   3. Abelard -- compromise -- conceptualism
      a. "Mankind" explains "Men"
      b. Authorities differ? Truth? Use reason
      c. St. Bernard replies

F. Scholasticism
   1. Averroes on Aristotle's Metaphysics
      a. Physical world, soul of mankind
      b. Individual salvation possible? Christian
         dogma?
   2. Albertus Magnus, founder and teacher
   3. Thomas Aquinas
      a. Summa Theologica -- Summa contra Gentiles
      b. Discuss God, Man, universe, authority
      c. Thomism: problem, 2 sides, answer, proof
      d. Faith plus reason -- the Truth above Nature
      e. Example: the children of Eden

G. Political Thought
   1. John of Salisbury, Policraticus, most typical
      a. "Organic" theory of society -- order & rank
      b. Equality souls -- dignity & worth all vo-
         cations
      c. Compromise -- perfection impossible on earth
      d. Moderation -- not totalitarianism

2. Aquinas -- follows Aristotle -- moderation
   a. State necessary evil -- good king best
   b. Limited monarchy, papal temporal authority
3. Marsiglio of Padua, <u>Defensor Pacis</u>
   a. True authority -- <u>The universitas civium</u>
   b. Not popular sovereignty -- "Organic" theory
4. Law -- Natural Law and custom
   a. Law to be found, not made
   b. Ethical, what "ought to be", reasonable
   c. Word of God, from Church and ancestors
   d. Common sense of community, plus special skills
   e. Static universe, perfection only in heaven
   f. Comparison medieval, modern outlook

H. Mysticism
   1. St. Bernard, St. Francis
      a. Distrust reason, intellect, books
      b. Christ's way -- submission both body & mind
   2. Bonaventura, <u>Voyage of the Mind to God</u>
      a. Reason -- the physical world
      b. Love -- mystical union with divine

I. Science
   1. Experimental method
      a. Roger Bacon, Abelard of Bath, Grosseteste
      b. Arab science studied, experimentation
   2. Progress in arts and crafts
      a. Farming, mining, metallurgy
      b. Clocks, optics, compass
   3. Scientific methods used
      a. Falconry, astrology, alchemy
      b. Intellectual discipline in Scholasticism
      c. Churchmen, authority, logic, facts
   4. Arab mathematics studied

TERMS, PEOPLE, EVENTS

Town charter
Craft guild
just price
usury
fair
Champagne fair
bourg, burgh, borg
bourgeois, burgesses, burghers
law merchant
Papal monarchy
canon law
Pope Gelasius I
Otto III
Henry III
Henry VI
Innocent III
teutonici
ministeria les class
allodial nobility
Investiture Controversy
Pope Leo IX
Pope Gregory VII
Hildebrand
"Go to Canossa"
Concordate of Worms
particularism
Guelf and Ghibeline
Frederick Barbarossa
The Italian Question
Italian communes
Lombard League
regalia question
Peace of Constance
Frederick II

Cluniac movement
Augustinians
Cistercians
conversi
St. Bernard
St. Francis
Dominicans
Franciscans
Apostles
trivium, quadrivium
Monastic school
Cathedral school
University
College
Bologna
Town and gown
nominalists
realists
Peter Abelard
Thomas Aquinas
Thomism
John of Salisbury
"Organic" theory
Marsiglio of Padua
Law of Nature
Bonaventure
Voyage of the Mind to God
Roger Bacon
Scholasticism
St. Dominic
Lateran Council of 1215
Interregnum
Civil war in Germany (1197-
12-15)

1. Describe and discuss the revival of towns under these headings: (a) causes; (b) government and law; (c) effect of towns on kings, the nobility, the serfs; (d) new economic institutions which developed; and (e) economic philosophy of the new cash economy.

2. Describe and discuss the Investiture Controversy under these headings; (a) define term "lay investiture"; (b) Why German princes wanted the right; (c) Why papacy opposed; (d) role of German nobility, Italian communes, various non-German rulers; (d) "weapons" of the emperor and the church; (f) the "final" settlement.

3. Describe and discuss the rise of "Papal Monarchy" and the problems involved in the involvement of the popes in Italian and Empire politics.

4. Explain how the involvement of the German emperors in non-German foreign affairs gradually forced the emperors to make concessions in Germany which led to real feudalism, serfdom, disunity, and particularism there.

5. Discuss and evaluate the statement that Frederick II was the "most interesting monarch of the middle ages."

6. Describe and discuss reform of the Church under these headings: (a) causes; (b) papal reform under Leo IX and Gregory VII; (c) monastic reform and problems; (d) impact of philosophers; and (e) reforms suggested by Frederick II.

7. Compare and contrast the orders of Friars with the older monastic orders in aims, methods, organization, impact, and other results.

8. Describe the role of the Church and the clergy as the center of intellectual life in the middle ages, especially their role in education, thought, preservation of the classics, and science.

9. Describe and discuss the philosophical system of Thomas Aquinas, his political ideas, and his solution of the conflict between faith and reason.

10. Explain the "Organic" theory of society and how it re-
    lated to class status, government, vocations, human
    nature, and its general view of life.

11. Describe, discuss, and evaluate the philosophical con-
    troversy between the "nominalists" and the "realists"
    over universal ideas, with many examples.

12. Compare and contrast (and evaluate) the differences be-
    tween the medieval and the modern way of looking at the
    universe, life, the solution of problems, law and au-
    thority.

Chapter 8

Medieval Western Society:

National Monarchy, Secular Literature and the Arts

This chapter continues the study begun in Chapter 7 of the struggle of the centralized government to emerge from the decentralization of the Feudal Age. We shall see how the monarchies of France and England, strengthened by such factors as a rising middle class, were largely successful in this endeavor, whereas the rulers of Germany and the Empire, as we have seen, largely failed to achieve a strong central government, despite promising beginnings. All three faced the opposition of the feudal nobility; all had both great and foolish monarchs; and all were confronted by the power of the Papal monarchy and the consequent struggle between the forces of Church and State, but both the French and English monarchy were able to resist or to ally themselves with these forces and so keep and strengthen their own powers.

In addition, we shall examine the development of the national administration of taxes, the courts, the system of justice, and the legal systems of both France and England in the period. We shall observe the growth of institutions of representative government in both countries in the Estates General of France and the Parliament of England. We shall consider the factors which made it possible for the kings of France to emerge with their powers virtually unchecked by the Estates General, while in England there was to develop the right of the various classes to be heard and their duties and obligations controlled by law, as can be seen in that great document of the age, the Magna Carta.

Finally, we shall scan the main threads of the vernacular literature of the priod in the west.

I. Introduction

    A. Nationality stereotypes
      1. How such assumptions might be made
      2. Current events, "Relevant" past to "prove" these

    B. Need for long view, knowledge of medieval history

II. The Development of France (987-1314)
    A. France in 987 under Hugh Capet
      1. How he became king -- why nobility support
      2. Relations with his great feudal vassals
      3. Partnership with the Church

    B. Developments after Hugh Capet (in monarchy)
      1. Succession policy -- stability of -- 1180
        altered
      2. Good relations, partnership, with Church
      3. Quiet growth royal authority, centralization
        a. Increased power over <u>curia regis</u>
        b. New classes, new royal officials
        c. <u>Prevots</u>, local administration
        d. Capetian alliance with middle class

    C. Contest with Normans (Angevin Empire)
      1. Growth power, land of Normans
        a. Centralization of administration of Normandy
        b. Conquest of England (1066)
        c. Marriages add land and power
        d. English, French holdings by 1154
      2. Philip Augustus and John of England
        a. Philip -- personality, appearance
        b. His policies to weaken English monarchy
        c. Use of legal powers as John's suzerain
          John's foolish marriage -- results
          Battle of Bouvines (1214)
          peace treaty (1259) and territory gained
      3. Philip Augustus and Albigensians
        a. Albigensians -- theology, ideas, areas,
          classes
        b. Church proclaims heresy -- Crusade
          Role nobility in early period
          Philip, Louis VII, the Inquisition
        c. Languedox, Toulouse added to royal lands

D. Royal Administration
1. Philip Augustus and royal authority
   a. Financial, military, judicial powers
   b. Church aid, interdict, with disruptive vassals
   c. Policies with marriages, remarriage of ladies
   d. New officials: bailli, seneschal
      Powers of prevots curtailed
      Bailli traval, not hereditary, no land
2. Louis IX and the bailli
   a. New enqueteurs, supervise bailli
   b. King gets fees, dues, supplies justice
3. Changes in Curia Regis (King's court)
   a. Reasons for growth -- sub-courts created
   b. High judicial tribunal -- parlement
      Trained lawyers -- rule in king's name
      Parlement de Paris -- central court
   c. Chambre des comptes, for finances
      Sources of revenue for king (six)
      King and direct tax limit

E. Louis IX (Saint Louis)
1. Basis of greatness
   a. Personal, family, religious life
   b. Relations with Church, popes, French clergy
2. Class conflict in towns -- Intervention
   a. Why Louis intervened
   b. His solutions to problems
3. Assertions of royal prerogatives
   a. New ordonnance without vassals' consent
   b. Examples: private wars, royal money
4. Royal justice
   a. Traditional types -- new pleas for
   b. Reputation for justice -- foreign appeals
5. Evaluation

F. Philip IV (Philip the Fair)
1. Background
   a. Philip as "typical" of western kings
   b. compared with Louis IX
      Ruthlessness, harshness (gens du roi)
      Hardening of traditional forces
      Failure of traditional checks
2. Royal justice
   a. Swallowing of feudal justice
   b. prevention; defaute de droit; faux jugement
   c. Changing role of parlement -- 3 new chambres

          specialization, professionalization
          More travel, extension of "justice"
    3. Changes in curia regis
       a. Secret council -- full council
       b. Estates General -- causes -- classes in
    4. War with English, finances, new ways to tax
    5. Philip the Fair and the Papacy
       a. Boniface VIII
       b. First clash (issues, acts, outcome)
       c. Second clash -- causes
             Pope's letter -- Philip's response
             Bull Unam Sanctam -- death of Boniface
       d. Babylonian Captivity (1305-1378)
             meaning -- results
    6. Philip and other "vested" interests
       a. Knights Templars, Jews, Italian bankers
       b. What done -- why -- results
    7. Protest against royal power
       a. Taxpayers revolt of 1314 -- Louis X response
       b. Unique rights in taxation kept

III. England, from the Anglo-Saxons to Edward I

  A. Norman Conquest
    1. England, Normandy compared in 1066
       a. Government, national and local
       b. Army, nobility -- Church, clergy
       c. Economy, commerce
       d. Education, intellectual life, monasteries
    2. Relations (England and Normandy) before 1066
       a. Queen Emma and other Norman ties, intrigues
       b. Edward the Confessor and William of Normandy
       c. Harold & William -- rival claims -- papacy
    3. Battle of Hastings (1066) and results
       a. Further conquest, pacification to 1071
       b. Treatment of English -- different views of
    4. Policies of William I after 1066
       a. Old English customs and laws kept
             Church, clergy -- castles, fyrd, Danegeld
             Sheriffs -- courts
       b. Norman feudal structure, nobility, super-
             imposed
             Salisbury Oath -- curia regis role
       c. Domesday Book -- thoroughness -- resentment
             from
       d. Relations with the papacy
       e. Monasteries -- learning -- Latin introduced

B. Henry I and Henry II
   1. Centralization under Henry I
      a. Salaried administrators, clergy officials
      b. New departments (chancery, exchequer)
      c. Small council (Privy Council) of curia regis
      d. Scutage use -- town taxation changes
   2. Anarchy over succession
   3. Henry II's policies
      a. End feudal anarchy
      b. New sources, methods of revenue
      c. Reorganization legal system, laws
         Old laws -- common law -- case law
         writes; juries; royal judges; grand juries
         treasury income -- system of evidence,
            proof
   4. Henry II and Becket
      a. Constitution of Clarendon proposed
         criminious clerics issue
         opposing positions on
      b. Papal appeal -- Becket murder -- penance
      c. Canon law over royal courts -- benefit of
         clergy
   5. Reorganization of fyrd

C. Richard I and John
   1. Financial problems of Richard I
      a. Why income needed -- methods -- severity of
      b. Bureaucracy growth -- results for John
   2. John and Pope Innocent III
      a. Issue -- use of interdict, excommunication
      b. Impact of French war on conflict
      c. John surrenders -- feudal vassal of pope
   3. John and the English barons
      a. Royal taxes, trials -- impact -- results
      b. Magna Carta (1215)
         Concessions to barons; towns; clergy;serfs
         Importance? Meaning then; growth; now
   4. John after Magna Carta
      a. John & the pope vs. barons and Archbishop
      b. French invade -- John death -- uneasy peace

D. Henry III and the Barons (1216-1272)
   1. Original good relations -- causes discord
   2. Provisions of Oxford -- Henry, pope response
   3. Civil war (causes, factions, results)

E. Growth of Parliament
   1. Importance

2. Background, terms (Norman, French, English)
   a. <u>Parlement</u> -- witenagemot -- councils
   b. <u>Aid and consel</u> -- duty and privilege
3. Growth baron discontent, demand for parliament
4. Knights of Shire, Burgesses
   a. Classes represented, strength, demands
   b. Why called -- when -- who
   c. Simon de Montfort, Parliament of 1265

F. Edward I
   1. Unification attempt -- Wales -- Scotland
   2. Edward the law-giver
      a. Statutes -- new spirit of -- types
      b. Growth specialized courts
   3. Trade duties -- importance of -- Jews
   4. Military duty and practices
      a. Distraint of knighthood
      b. Confirmation of <u>Magna Carta</u> in 1297
   5. Model Parliament of 1295
      a. Classes in -- assertions of powers & rights
      b. "What touches all should be approved by all"

G. England and France compared
   1. Powers of king and crown
   2. Restraints, powers of nobility
   3. Crown and law, grants
   4. Importance of growth of Parliament in England

IV. Literature in the Medieval West

A. BAckground
   1. Eleventh century as turning point
   2. Importance of Latin continues
      a. Church, education, learned men
      b. Law, politics, documents
      c. Sermons, hymns, verse, Goliardic songs

B. Vernacular triump in France
   1. Epics, songs, song-cycles of north
      a. Chivalry of fighting man
      b. <u>Song of Roland</u> -- King Arthur -- Trojan wars
   2. Lyric love poetry, courtly love, in south
      a. Troubadours -- artificial and formal code
      b. Aquitaine -- Eleanor and her "court"
   3. Saint Louis and the Fourth Crusade

C. Vernacular in Italy
   1. Palermo court of Frederick II, love poetry

2. Dante Alighieri
   a. The Divine Comedy -- place, importance of
   b. Medieval moral and ethic ideals from
3. Petrarch, Boccaccio (See later sections)

D. Chaucer and Middle English
   1. His life, career, other works
   2. Canterbury Tales
      a. Themes -- why typical medieval
      b. Stories from

TERMS, PEOPLE, EVENTS

Hugh Capet
Capetians
Angevin Dynasty
Philip II, Philip Augustus
Battle of Bouvines
Albigensian Heresy
Albigensian Crusade
Louis IX, Saint Louis
Sieur de Joinville
Philip IV (Philip the Fair)
Estates General
Boniface VIII
Unan Sanctam
papal bull
Babylonian Captivity
curia regis
prevots
bailli and seneschal
parlement
Parlement de Paris
ordonnance
gens du roi
interdict
Norman Conquest
Battle of Hastings
William I (William the Conqueror
fyrd
Dangegeld
sheriff
Salisbury Oath
Domesday Book
scutage
chancery
exchequer
common law

writs
juries
royal justice
grand jury
trial by ordeal
Constitution of Clarendon
Thomas Becket
benefit of clergy
common consent of the realm
Harold
Henry I
Henry II
Richard the Lionhearted
John
Henry III
Edward I
John and Innocent III
Magna Carta
Archbishop Stephen Langton
Provisions of Oxford
witenagemot
aid and consel
knights of the shire
burgesses
Simon de Montfort
Parliament of 1265
Model Parliament
Parliament
Edward I and Scotland
Robert Bruce
Battle of Bannockburn
Statute of Mortmain
distraint of knighthood
Edward the law-giver
Chansons de Geste

Goliardic songs
Song of Roland
Eleanor of Aquitaine
chivalry
courtoisie
song cycles
troubadours
Dante Alighieri
The Divine Comedy
Geoffrey Chaucer
Canterbury tales

SAMPLE QUESTIONS

1. Describe and discuss the changes in the system of local and national administration in France under Hugh Capet, Philip II Augustus, Louis IX, and Philip the Fair.

2. Do the same thing for royal justice. Discuss the kinds of law, courts, judges and the role of the crown in both local and national law and justice.

3. Describe and discuss the Albigensian heresy and Crusade, mentioning the causes, chief ideas, chief events, role of the nobility and the king, the religious and non-religious issues, and the results.

4. Describe, discuss, and evaluate the reputation in both formal history and legend of:
    a. Louis IX of France,
    b. King John of England, and
    c. Edward I (The Law-giver) of England.

5. Compare and contrast Louis IX and Philip the Fair.

6. Describe and discuss the issues, chief events, and the results of the struggle between king Philip the Fair of France and Pope Boniface VIII.

7. Describe and discuss the national administrative system introduced into England by William the Conqueror.

8. Describe and discuss the changing relationship, powers, and duties of the king, the barons, and the towns in England from the time of Edward the Confessor to Henry III and mention the witenagemot, curia regis, the early parliaments, and the growth of the parliament to the

Model Parliament of 1295.

9. Describe and discuss the causes, chief events, and the results of the struggle between Henry II and Thomas Becket.

10. Describe, discuss, and evaluate the chief provisions of Magna Carta about the barons, the towns, the Church, and the clergy.

11. Discuss and evaluate the original meaning of the above provisions of Magna Carta, the change in the meaning of these provisions, and the long-range implications.

12. Compare and contrast Henry II and his sons, Richard the Lionhearted and John.

13. Describe, discuss, and evaluate the changes in England of royal justice. Mention the system of law, the kinds of law, the kinds of courts, juries, writs, the role of the sheriff, and the judges.

14. Compare and contrast the methods used by the French and the English kings to obtain royal income. Show how the success or failure of their efforts had much to do with the growth of the crown and/or the power of the barons.

15. Compare and contrast the parlement of France and the parliament of England.

16. Compare and contrast the knightly chivalry of the man on horseback and the chivalry of courtly love and of "courtoisie".

17. Compare and contrast the writings of Dante and Chaucer, showing how they were both products of medieval ideas and ideals, yet how they differed.

Chapter 9

The East: Late Middle Ages

In this second of two chapters on the East during the Middle Ages, the pre-eminence of Byzantium comes gradually to an end; the proud and supremely confident leader of civilization, surrounded by but always repelling "barbarian" dangers, falters and collapses.

The conservatism of Byzantium's state and church and the static character of its society no doubt reduced the effectiveness with which it faced the more dynamic peoples who now pressed forward from both the West and the East. At the beginning of this period, the West sent armies of Crusaders to assist Byzantium in repelling a new wave of Moslem expansion from the east, now under the vigorous leadership of the Turks. Then these western "Franks" gained control of Syria and Palestine and even founded new western-style states there, but eventually they lost both these states and also their temporary conquest of the city of Byzantium as well. Byzantium never recovered from this lesson of western military superiority and, handicapped further by internal weaknesses, was conquered piecemeal by the Ottoman Turks in the fourteenth and fifteenth centuries.

But the heritage of Byzantium lived on, partly in the cultural contributions made to the West, but also in the two successor states, the Ottoman Empire and Muscovite Russia. Both would later raise the claim that they were the true and only heir to Byzantium. The history of these two states is carried in this chapter beyond the limits of the Middle Ages to the end of the seventeenth century to the time when the Ottoman state began to decline and Russia became one of the great powers of Europe. This is done to keep the key of the textbook to the study of the East: its separate development and yet its unity with the total of the story of Western Civilization and its connections with western Europe.

TOPIC OUTLINE

I. Main Threads of Period

    A. Crisis for Byzantium (Eleventh century)
      1. Norman and Muslim invasion dangers
      2. Venetian alliance and aid

    B. Crusades (1095-1291)
      1. Areas, leadership, routes, results
      2. Relationships

    C. Downfall of Byzantium
      1. Crusades, Venice, Genoa, Serb influence
      2. Ottoman influence, conquest

    D. Ottoman Turks, successors to Byzantium
      1. Balkans, then Constantinople captured (1453)
      2. Fusion with Byzantium, becomes successor state

    E. Post-Kiev Russia as Byzantine successor state
      1. Kiev decline; Rise Poland, Lithuania, Novgorod
      2. Tatar rule -- Muscow rise; Muscow as Third Rome

II. The Crusades

    A. Background, previous movements
      1. Old idea of reconquest of Holy Land by holy war
      2. Pilgrimages; salvation, relics
      3. Safe passage ended by Ottoman conquest of Asia
         Minor
      4. Pope Gregory VII: Crusade to end East-West
         Schism

    B. First Crusade
      1. Pope Urban II calls
        a. Byzantium needs aid -- Council of Clarmont
        b. Religious, material, political motives
      2. Two armies
        a. Peter the Hermit and his peasant "army"
           Who went -- progress of -- motives
           Byzantium impact -- final results
        b. Regular, feudal army
           Who went -- progress -- leaders -- impact
           Byzantine response -- Conquests by 1099
      3. Four Crusader States
        a. Locations -- leaders -- role of Italian cities
        b. Political, religious government -- disunity

4. Three Military Orders
    a. Why established -- how -- aims -- vows --
       deeds
    b. Historical development, changes -- final end

C. Second Crusade
    1. Causes -- role of St. Bernard, kings
    2. Rise of Saladin -- results -- causes failure

D. Other Crusades
    1. Third Crusade (1189-1192)
        a. Three famous kings in -- Byzantium response
        b. Death of Saladin -- results -- why failure

    2. Fourth Crusade
        a. Innocent III's role -- Diverted to Byzantium
        b. Results -- new states -- Byzantine decline
    3. European crusades, papal campaigns
        a. Success in Spain
        b. Teutonic Knights in Baltic
        c. Albigensian Crusade (1208-1240)
        d. Papal forces vs. Frederick II (1220-1250)
    4. Children's Crusade of 1212
    5. Other crusades against Muslims in Near East
        a. Fifth Crusade, to Egypt
        b. Frederic II -- diplomatic -- Treaty of 1229
           Christian, Muslim response
           Jerusalem retaken (1244), held to 1917
        c. Saint Louis' 2 crusades (1249, 1270)
    6. Mamluks reconquer Near East, North Africa by
       1291

E. Results of the Crusades
    1. On few who stayed in the east -- fusion
    2. On the many who returned -- their influence
        a. Economic -- products, trade, business methods
        b. Urbanization speeded up -- agrarian changes
        c. Political -- impact on feudalism, nobles,
           kings
        d. Religious -- papacy, clergy, hatred of
           Muslims
        e. Culture -- poetry, geography
        f. Crusaders: over-seas religious colonists?

III. The Fortunes of the Byzantine Empire, 1081-1453

A. Western influences
    1. Trade take-over by Italians

2. Military domination by Crusaders
3. Growth of mutual hatred, suspicion

B. Internal decay
1. Victory of the "powerful" -- results
2. Localism, feudalism -- proncia growth
3. Economic ruin, misery, taxes, corruption

C. Fourth Crusade
1. Venice diverts -- family strife for throne
2. Zara, Constantinopel taken - Papal response
3. Broken promises, fire, revolt, siege, diaster

D. Latin Empire (1203-1261)
1. What it was -- causes
2. Baldwin as emperor -- Venetial patriarch
3. New feudal states, old western feudal customs
4. Bulgarian, Greek response -- recapture in 1261

E. Byzantium after 1261
1. Michael VIII -- diplomacy of -- Sicily
2. His successors -- war for throne -- social
   strife
3. Theological controversy -- economic chaos
4. Serbs, Bulgarians, Genoa, Venice interfere

F. The Advance of the Ottoman Turks
1. Synthesis of Ottoman, Turk, Byzantine elements
2. Gradual conquest of Asia Minor and Balkans
   a. Constantinople surrounded -- relations with
   b. Timur attack puts off final disaster
3. Final conquest (1453) -- Good relations with
   Greeks
4. Cooperation with Orthodox church

IV. The Ottoman Successor-State, 1453-1699

A. Inheritances: Asian, Persian, Byzantine, Muslim

B. The Ottoman System
1. Political, religious role of conquered peoples
2. The Sultans -- Vital importance of
3. The Administrators (4 subdivisions) All slaves
   a. Men of the emperor, the imperial class
      Devshirme recruits to balance -- source
      Education, advancement -- Other uses
   b. Men of the sword
      Cavalrymen (spahis) with land grants

Infantry (<u>yenicheri</u>) from <u>devshirme</u>
Army size, ability, prestige
c. Men of the pen
d. Sages (judges, teachers, scholars, muftis)
   Mufti, apply law of Islam
   Importance of Grand Mufti (<u>Sheikh-ul-Islam</u>)
4. Causes loss of viogor of system
   a. Sultans weak, factions; harem intrigue
   b. Mufti & changeless law, so no development

C. Ottoman expansion to 1566
   1. Asia Minor and Balkans to 1460
   2. Further expansion
      a. Black Seas area
      b. Sultan Selim I's conquests
   3. Suleiman the Magnificant
      a. Western European contemporary men, events
      b. Threat to Europe, place in conflicts
      c. Hungary, Vienna -- Africa -- Middle East
      d. Treaty of 1536 with France; terms; significance

D. Ottoman Decline
   1. Causes
      a. Internal: sultans, localism, simony, revenue
      b. External: stronger, equal European powers
   2. Events
      a. Lepanto in 1571
      b. Murad IV, Koprulu viziers revival
      c. Vienna agains -- Ukraine
   3. End of an Era
      a. Karlovitz congress of 1699
      b. Military decline -- defensive diplomacy
      c. Greek domination of diplomacy, administration

V. Russia from 1200 to 1700

   A. Results of collapse Kievan Russia in 1200
      1. Uncertain future, leadership
      2. Which of four regions, spirits?
         a. South -- Liev
         b. West -- Lithuania, Poland -- feudalism, manors
            Roman Catholicism -- western ties
         c. North -- Novgorod -- commercial oligarchy, rigid classes, merchants & <u>veche</u>

-111-

       d. Moscow -- strong prince -- merchants, nobles
          not strong -- good agriculture

B. Tatars in Russia
  1. Conquest -- areas, reasons for success
  2. European contacts to aid against Muslims
  3. System in Russia (The Golden Horde)
    a. Absence of local control, occupation
    b. Tribute main concern -- Moscow most affected
  4. Tatar impact on Russian civilization
    a. Good or bad? Evidence, role of Moscow
    b. Concensus -- a serious calamity

C. Development of Muscovite State
  1. Advantages of Moscow
    a. Geography -- trade
    b. Able princes -- marriages, land, succession
    c. Role against Tatars
    d. Support of Orthodox Dhurch, partnership
  2. Ivan III and autocracy
    a. National, religious war & crisis for 200 years
    b. Feudalism, nobility -- no unity
    c. Church ideology, hystorical mythology
       Heir of Byzantium, Kiev, Rome (Rurik)
       Unlimited power from God -- autocrat, czar
       Religious justification of royal practices
  3. Changing Nobles and Serfs (1462-1689)
    a. Merger of old and new nobility
       Estates, titles, state services due
       Gradual elimination of differences
    b. Peasants become serfs
       War, chaos, debt -- so hereditary tie to
         land
       Major characteristic of later Russia
       Typical of how western ideas came to
         Russia
  4. Reign of Ivan the Terrible
    a. Early life -- personality -- how it affected
       him
    b. Period of sound government, reform
       Supervision of imperial administrators
       Zemski sobor (character; compared with
         west)
    c. Illness -- oprichnina -- the oprichniks
    d. Eastern expansion -- Volga watershed
  5. The Time of Troubles
    a. Earlier indications of coming events

b. Rival czars -- plague, famine -- civil war
c. Foreign domination -- war -- Poles expelled
6. The _Zemski sobor_ and Czar Michael Romanov
   a. _Zemski sobor_ -- Romanov as elected autocrat
   b. Move towards parliamentary government
   c. Gradual discontinuation of use of _zemski_
      sobor
   d. Government under theRomanovs
      National bureaus, ministries, departments
      Provinces, local government --opposition
      Frequent serf revolts -- Stenka Razin
7. Role of the Church in Russia
   a. Partnership with autocracy
      Czar appointment of patriarch
      Two experiments in dyarchy
   b. Church, literature, and the arts
      Kinds of literature -- theological writings
      Role of Old Church Slavonic
      Absence of vernacular, secular literature
8. Expansion of Russia
   a. Role of Cossacks -- misconceptions about
   b. Direction, opponents of expansions
9. Russia and the West
   a. Slow penetration during whole period
      Foreigners who came -- where -- when
      Trade, ideas from -- Russian travel abroad
      Russian response to foreigners,their ideas
   b. Depp religious impact of new ideas --
      opponents

VI. Conclusions

TERMS, PEOPLE, EVENTS

Crusaders
Urban II
First Crusade (1095-1099)
Teutonic Knights
Hospitallers
Second Crusade (1143-1149)
Innocent II and the Crusades
Children's Crusade (1212)
Saint Louis' Crusades
Baldwin of Loraine
proncia
mufti
Selim I
Congress of Karlovitz (1699)
Battles of Lepanto, Kossovo,
   Mohacs, Vienna (2)
Polish-Lithuanian State
veche
Third Rome
Czar; autocrat
zemski sobor
Ivan the Terrible
The Time of Troubles
Stenka Razin
Old Church Slavonic

Council of Clermont (1095)
Peter the Hermit
Crusader States
Templars
Saladin
Third Crusade (1189-11-92)
Fourth Crusade (1202-1204)
Frederick II's Crusade
Latin Empire (1204-1261)
Ottoman Turks
Devshirme
Sheikh-ul-Islam
Suleiman the Magnificent
Koprulu viziers
Tatars
The Golden Horde
Novgorod
Principality of Moscow
Ivan III
Service nobility
boyars
oprichina
Michael Romanov
Old Believers
Cossacks

Locate these bodies of water:
Mediterranean, aegean, Adriatic, Baltic, Black,
Caspian, and Azov Seas.
Lake Ilmen.
Dniester, Dneiper, Don, Volga, Danube, and Sava
Rivers.

Locate these cities:
Vienna, Buda, Pest, Belgrade, Genoa, Venice, Zara,
Ragusa, Durazzo, Marseille, Tunis, Thessalonica,
Adrianople, Constantinople, Nicomedia, Nicaea,
Iconium (Konia), Edessa, Baghdad, Antioch, Tripoli,
Tyre, Acre, Damascus, Jerusalem, Damietta, Cairo,
Limasol, Kiev, Moscow, Novgorod, Sarai, and Azov.

Locate these areas:
Crimea, Ukraine, Lithuania, Poland, Teutonic Knights
holdings, Pland, Sweden, Hungary, the Holy Roman
Empire, Transylvania, Moldavia, Podolia, Wallachia,
Bosnia, Serbia, Montenegro, Bulgaria, Macedonia,
Arabia, Syria, Anatolia, Mesopotamia, Persia, Egypt,
Crete, Rhodes, and Cyprus.

Locate these battles;
Kossovo, Mohacs, Lepanto, Vienna.

Locate the Empire of Venice.

Locate the 4 Crusader States.

Trace the routes of the various Crusades

Show Ottoman expansion from 1481, 1481-1520, 1520-1566,
1566-1683, and the tributary states.

Show Russian expansion with Tatar dominions in 1300, the
Principality of Moscow in 1300, Russia in 1505, and
in 1689.

SAMPLE QUESTIONS

1. Describe, discuss, and evaluate th4e various internal
   and external factors which led to the decline and final
   collapse of the Byzantine Empire. Which do you think
   was most important? Why?

2. Describe and discuss the rise of the Ottoman Empire, its
   major institutional features, the internal and external
   reasons for its decline, and its impact on European
   civilization.

3. Comment: The Ottoman state was the successor of both
   the Islamic world and the old Byzantine Empire.

4. Describe, discuss, and evaluate the causes, chief events,
   and results of the First Crusade.

5. Do the same for the Fourth Crusade.

6. Do the same for the Crusades (all together) as a whole.

7. Describe, discuss, and evaluate the evidence for and
   against the view that the Crusades were almost entirely
   religious in nature.

8. Describe, discuss, and evaluate the factors which led to
   the predominance of Moscow in Russia, rather than Kiev,
   the Polish-Lithuanian state, or Novgorod.

9. Describe, discuss, and evaluate the impact of the Tatar
   domination of Russia on the future of Russia.

10. Describe, discuss, and evaluate the impact of Byzantium
    upon Russia.

11. Describe and discuss the development of autocracy in
    Russia.

12. Explain why the zemski sobor did not develop in the same
    way as did similar insitituions in western Europe.

13. Compare and contrast the role of the church in the three
    Romes.

14. Describe and discuss the development of the nobility
    and the serfs in Moscovite Russia.

15. Describe and discuss the development of the unusual relationship between church and state in Russia.

16. Describe, discuss, and evaluate the impact of both foreigners and foreign ideas on Russia in the period.

17. Comment: Together with the absolute autocracy, the institution of serfdom is the most characteristic feature of Russian society.

18. Comment: Long after the West had emerged from the Middle Ages -- in fact, down to the end of the seventeenth century -- the Ottoman Empire and Russia were still medieval.

Chapter 10

The West: War and Politics in the Late Middle Ages

By the end of the fourteenth century, certain trends
had developed in all western European states which seemed
to present the danger that war, chaos, and anarchy might
upset the illusions of the stability of the Feudal Age.
Clear and conflicting interest groups had emerged and become aware of their separate and conflicting social, economic, and political aspirations. The king, nobility, clergy,
and towns seemed to face inevitable chaos, war, and conflict. Revolt of the serfs and unskilled town laborers
seemed just as imminent. Compounding these manifestations
of impending chaos was the presence within each group of
internal interests which might render any particular group
easy prey for the others: struggles between rival factions
and families for the throne, between the new and the old
nobility, between the papacy and the national clergy, between the high and low clergy, between the major and the
minor guilds, between the country gentry and the nobility,
and between the rural and urban interests of each class and
group. In addition, each group might have factional strife
over national or international objectives, between older
chivalrous or bastard feudalistic outlooks, and even over
the special family and dynastic interests of particular
individuals. In Spain, the continuaiton of the crusading
movement compounded the issue even moer.

Such a list of conflicting interests -- and more could
be added -- may seem confusing. But, if one is aware of the
complicating interests within each group, a simple explana-
tion is impossible. Awareness of the strengths and weaknesses of each factor in each western nation make the triumph
of a single solution for all of Europe just as impossible.
And if one is aware of the ever-present factor of mere
blind chance in history, then the idea that the final solution was somehow the inevitable working out of some
national genius or mission is absurd. What if! Suppose
that Henry V had lived a long life, that Henry VI had been
stronger, that Louis XI had been weaker, or that the Black
Death had not confused an already muddied puddle?

In any case, combinations of these factors led to the
triumph of a strong central monarchy in France, the partnership of Parliament and Crown in England, the change of particularism into local autonomy and sovereignty in Germany,

and a special harvest of despotism and naked power politics in Italy. Even the special factors of the religious zeal and a happy marriage alliance leading to a strong and intolerant national state in Spain was colored by most of these factors.

All in all, while each of these national workings-out of the common problems was special and different, the period has a central unity which is more than a mere illusion.

TOPIC OUTLINE

I. Introduction: The passage from medieval to modern

   A. East and West compared (When, where, why changes?)
   B. Symptoms of decline of medieval institutions
     1. Rigid and sterile attitudes
     2. Politics and Bastard feudalism
     3. Economic changes
     4. Chronic social strife -- rural and urban

   C. Significant traumatic events, their results.
     1. Great Famine (1315-1317)
     2. Black Death (1347-1350)

II. The Emerging National Monarchies

   A. The Hundred Years' War -- First Round (1337-1360)
     1. Causes
       a. Dispute over French throne -- Salic law
       b. Feudal rights in Aquitaine, Normandy, others
       c. Flanders, the cloth trade, class conflict
     2. Trends in France during the war
     3. English victories (when, where, why)
     4. France -- results of defeat
       a. Development of trends common to later history
       b. Estates General vs. Charles the Wise(issues)
       c. Marcel, Paris, the Jacquerie -- lessons of
       d. Why Charles the Wise won

   B. The Hundred Years' War -- Second Round (1369-1453)
     1. Early military, internal successes of Charles
     2. Civil War -- Burgundians vs. Armagnacs
       a. Royal policy of apranges -- results
       b. Causes immediate problem -- English role
     3. Truce: Treaty of Troyers (1420) -- terms of
       a. "A fantastic settlement"
       b. Possible results -- who supported
       c. Death of two kings prevents "success"
     4. Charles VII and Joan of Arc
       a. Joan of Arc -- career and death
       b. Peace with Burgundy -- Paris recovered
       c. Nobles revolt; the countryside, the "flayers"
     5. Reforms of Charles VII
       a. Standing army based on direct taxes(taille)
       b. Pragmatic Sanction of Bourges (1438)
            Terms of -- meaning -- Gallicanism
            Victory over papal power in France

C. France under Louis XI (1461-1483)
   1. Character of Louis XI -- Commynes on
      a. Compared with Charles the Bold of Burgundy
      b. His policies (taxes, papacy, army)
   2. The threat of Burgundy
      a. Background -- before Louis XI
         Land, wealth of Duke Philip the Good
         Philip, Charles VII, and the English
      b. Charles the Bold and unification
         Attempt to seize Alsace and Lorraine
         Swiss opposition, victory --death of
            Charles
      c. Partition of Burgundy -- later results
   3. Consolidation and reform
      a. End of appanages -- Armagnac faction beaten
      b. Bastard feudalism virtually dended
      c. Competent central admiinistration
   4. Evaluation his reign, the period, for France

D. England and the emergence of national monarchy
   1. General trends -- compared with France
   2. Edward II (1307-1327)
      a. Scotland, Bannockburn (1314) -- results
      b. Barons -- Ordinances of 1311 -- results
      c. Parliament repeals -- murder of the king
   3. Edward III (1327-1377)
      a. Military progress and victories
      b. Black Death impact -- labor -- food
         Statute of Laborers (1351) -- terms, re-
            sults
         Vision of Piers Plowman evidence on period
      c. Justices of the peace (JP's) emerge --
            future of
      d. Rise of national feeling
         Statutes of Provisors and Praemunire
         English language in court and school
      e. John Wiclif -- religious protest and
            nationalism
         Causes, ideas on proper church practices
         Bible translation
   4. Development of the Parliament
      a. Two houses -- membership -- clergy role
      b. Changing functions -- judicial -- financial
      c. Growth legislative powers -- important acts
   5. Richard II (1377-1399)
      a. Peasants' Revolt (1381)
            Causes -- Wiclif influence
            Main events -- results

        b. Bastard feudalism -- livery and maintenance
        c. Barons and growing private wars
            Factions; leaders; use of parliament
            Richard overthrown, murdered
   6. Lancaster and York (1399-1485) civil war
        a. Background -- causes -- bastard feudalism
            Need for stability -- line of weak
               kings
            Revolts -- private wars -- Parliament
               used
        b. Lancastrian kings, their reigns(1399-1461)
            Henry IV -- parliament conflict --
               revolts
            Henry V -- France won -- Wiclif follow-
               ers
            Henry VI -- France lost -- barons rule
        c. War of the Roses (1455-1485)
            Issues, factions, leaders, kings, events
            Yorkist kings -- Warwick and Parliament
            Richard III -- historical controversy
            Bosworth Field (1485) -- Richard III
               death
   7. Henry VII and the House of Tudor
        a. Character, claim to throne, qualifications
        b. Security of Tudor dynasty -- popularity
        c. Curb of nobility -- Court of Star Chamber
        d. New classes, officials, methods (Morton's
            Fork)
        e. Contributions, evaluation of Henry VII
        f. Policy towards Parliament, absolutism

E. Spain -- Ferdinand and Isabella (1479-1516)
   1. Compared with L ouis XI, Henry VII
   2. Reconquest of peninsula -- 500 year crusade
        a. Christian kingdoms (Castile, Portugal,
            Aragon)
        b. Limits on royal power
             Nobility, towns, clergy, Cortes,<u>Mesta</u>
            Strong regional loyalties
   3. Marriage alliance of Ferdinand & Isabella
        a. Personality of each -- aims -- policies
            Ferdinand, Aragon, Mediterranean
               policies
            Isabella, towns, <u>Mesta,</u> and the
               militia
        b. Consolidation of power
            Nobles, military brotherhoods suppressed

                    Alliance with the Church -- Cardinal
                       Ximenes -- Spanish Inquisition
                    Suppression of the Jews and Muslims
        4. Year 1492 as critical date in Spanish history
           a. Columbus voyage
           b. Granada fall -- intolerable nationalism

III. Particularism in Germany and Italy

    A. The Princes and the Empire
       1. Comparisons with France,England, Spain
       2. Interregnum (1254-1273) -- meaning -- results
          a. Princes complete usurpation
          b. Germany and Italy end links
       3. Rudolf of Hapsburg (1273-1291) as emperor
          a. Dynastic Hapsburg policies
          b. Emperor as territorial prince
       4. Golden Bull of 1356
          a. Elector system -- princes supreme -- Church
             role
          b. Local sovereign rights -- particularism
             complete

    B. The Princes and the Estates
       1. Threat of new fragmentation
          a. Nobles, towns, clergy -- taxes for privileges
          b. Growth free cities -- Hanse in north
          c. Anarchy -- robber barons -- private wars
       2. Consolidation of princely powers
          a. Golden Bull, Spread of Roman Law -- results
          b. Princes equal power of western kings
          c. Growing cooperation pf princes ande estates

    C. The Empire and Nationalism
       1. Emergining national feelings frustrated
          a. Emperor -- changing role of
             Hapsburgs as hereditary emperors -results
             Territorial and dynastic policy dominate
          b. Territorial losses from Empire
             Western lands to France
             Swiss Confederation breask away (1291)
       2. Maximilian I (1493-1519)
          a. Marriage policies -- leads to Charles V power
          b. Failure of reform

    D. Despots and Condottieri in Italy
       1. Background

                            -123-

      a. Growing national feeling -- no focus for
      b. Communes -- despots not traditional
          Republics run by commercial oligarchies
          Class war -- Guelfs and Ghibelline split
      c. Despots, <u>condottieri</u> to end chaos
          Famous examples
  2. Changing map of Italy -- predominance of 5 states
      a. Two sicilies
          Foreign domination continues -- Aragon,
            Spain
          Decline during period -- Naples excepted
      b. States of the Church
          Causes 14th and 15th century decline
          Great popes restore influence, glory
          Decline in Reformation, Dynastic Wars
      c. Milan
          Economic, strategic importance--government
          Heads Lombard League -- 12th century
            expansion
          Sforza family -- Lucovico Il Moro greatest
      d. Florence
          Economic importance -- government
          Major guilds, Guelf oligarchy -- lottery
          Minor guilds, <u>Ciompi</u> rivalry and revolt
          Medici family -- nature their despotism
          Cosimo, Lorenzo -- decline -- grand dukes
      e. Venice
          Compared with Milan and Florence
          Economic importance -- trade and the empire
          Commercial oligarchy -- Golden Book - doge
          Great Council, Council of Ten -- policies
  3. Italy as the "School of Europe"
      a. Meaning of term, examples
          Despots -- military affairs -- diplomacy
          Balance of Power -- results for Italy
      b. Niccolo Machiavelli
          <u>The Prince</u> -- human nature & power politics
          <u>Discourses</u> -- controversy and assessment

TERMS, PEOPLE, EVENTS

Bastard feudalism
Great Famine
Black Death
Hundred Years' War
Salic law
Valois kings
Etienne Marcel
Jacquerie
apanages
Burgundians
Armagnacs
Battle of Agincourt (1415)
Treaty of Troyers (1420)
Charles VII
Joan of Arc
flayers
taille
Jacques Coeur
Pragmatic Sanction of Bourges (1438)
Gallicanism
Louis XI and Charles the Bold
Commynes
Louis XI
Statute of Provisors (1351)
Statute of Praemunire (1353)
House of Lancaster
Edward II
Battle of Bannockburn
Ordinances of 1311
Lords ordainers
Edward III
Statute of Laborers
Piers Plowman
Justices of the peace
John Wiclif (Wycliffe)
House of Commons
House of Lords
country gentry
lords spiritual
knights of the shire
burgesses
magnates
Speaker of the House
Richard II
Peasants' Revolt (1381)

livery and maintenance
John of Gaunt
House of York
Henry IV
Henry V ("Prince Hal")
War of the Roses
Warwick the kingmaker
Edward IV
Richard III
The little princes
Edward V
Bosworth Field (1485)
Henry VII
House of Tudor
Court of Star Chamber
Morton's Fork
Tutor Absolutism
Mesta
Cortes
Ferdinand of Aragon
Isabella of Castile
Council of Castile
Cardinal Jimenex (Ximenes)
Spanish Inquisition
Suppression of the Jews and
    Muslims
The year 1492
Medici family
Sforza family
Council of ten
The School of Europe
The Prince
Interregnum (1254-1273)
Rudolf of Hapsburg
Golden Bull of 1356
Emperor Charles IV
Swiss Confederation (1291)
cantons
Maximilian I
Hanse
condottieri
Age of Despots
Guelfs vs. Ghibellines

Francesco Sforza
Visconti family
Ludovico II Moro
Sixus IV
Alexander VI
Cesare Borgia
Julius II
Borgia popes
Parlemento of Milan
Major, minor quilds
Guelf oligarchy
Commercial oligarchy
Great Council
Ciompi
doge
Golden Book
Niccolo Machiavelli
The Discourses

Locate these bodies of water:
Baltic, North, Mediterranean, and Adriatic Seas.

Locate these rivers: Rhine, Rhone, Arno, Po.

Locate these areas:
England, Scotland, Ireland, Wales, Flanders, Normandy,
Brittany, Alsac, Lorraine, Burgundy, Swiss Confedera-
tion, Aquitaine, Armagnac, Dauphine, Leon, Navarre,
Aragon, Castile, Portugal, Catalonia, Granada, Ba-
learic Islands, Corsica, Sardinia, Sicily, Crete,
Cyprus, Ionian Islands, Brandenburg, Saxony, Bohemia,
Palatinate, Venetian Empire, Kingdom of the Two
Sicilies, States of the Church, Ramagna, Lucca, Sienna,
Ferrara, Mantua, Tuscany, Genoa, Savoy, and Milan.

Locate these cities:
York, Lancaster, London, Oxford, Cambridge, Calais,
Troyers, Paris, Bourges, Reims, Avignon, Barcelona,
Toledo, Granada, Mainz, Trier, Naples, Pisa, Trieste,
Ravenna, Rome, Milan, Verrona, Bologna, Genoa, Turin,
Padua, Venice, Florence, Vienna.

Locate these battles:
Bosworth, Bannockburn, Agincourt, Cresy, Poitiers,
and Las Navas de Tolosa.

Show the Boundaries of the Empire.

NOTE: Some of the questions below have many parts and are given as examples of questions. In a test, it is likely that a student will be asked only a few parts of each.

1. Describe and discuss the causes, chief, events, and results of the Hundred Years' War. Explain especially why England won all of the important battles in the first phase of the war and yet eventually lost.

2. Describe and discuss the results of the early defeats in the Hundred Years' War on the monarchy, the nobility, and the towns. Be suer to explain the events which became "typical" of later French history.

3. Describe and discuss the Burgundian vs. Orleans-Armagnac conflict under these headings: (a) basic strengths and weakness of each side; (b) the role of nationalism; (c) the role of Joan of Arc; (d) the devices by which Charles VII gained the upper hand; and (e) the final results.

4. Explain the terms, nature, significance, and results of the Pragmatic Sanction of Bourges.

5. Describe and discuss the reign of Louis XI with specific reference to his character and its influence, his struggle with Charles the Bold, his relations with the Estate General, his relations with the towns, and the reasons for his ultimate triumph.

6. Describe and discuss the evolution of Parliament under these headings: (a) elements in the early Parliaments; (b) how and why two houses arose; (c) nature and membership of each house; (d) the original duties of the early Parliaments; (e) how and why these purposes were modified; and (f) the composition and purposes of Parliament by the time of Henry VII.

7. Describe, discuss, and evaluate the nature and significance of the Peasants' Revolt and the heresy of Wiclif in the reign of Richard II. Mention specific parts of the ideas of Wiclif.

8. Describe, discuss, and evaluate the causes, chief events, and results of the Lancaster-York struggle.

9. Describe and discuss the reign of Henry VII under these headings: (a) how he became king; (b) his character and chief policies; (c) how he eliminated or neutralized his opposition; (d) how he won support and popularity; and (e) his relations with Parliament.

10. Describe and discuss Spain in the period under these headings: (a) the leading areas in about 1450; (b) the significance of the religious problem; (c) the marriage between Ferdinand and Isabella; (d) their relations with the nobility; (e) with the towns; (f) with the Church; (g) with the Moslems and Jews; (h) significance of the year 1492; and (i) nature of Spain after 1492.

11. Describe and discuss Germany in the period under these headings: (a) nature and results of the Interregnum; (b) causes and results of the struggle over imperial policy; (c) rise of the Hapsburgs and their policies; (d) reign of Maximilian I; (e) the terms and results of the Golden Bull of 1356; (f) the three threats to the princes and how each was eliminated; and (g) the significance of the rise of the free cities.

12. Describe and discuss Italy in the period under these headings: (a) the situation in each of the five states in about 1250 (government, leadership, groups); (b) how, why, when, and where despots or condottieri arose; (c) some of the most famous of these; (d) differences in development in Milan, Venice, and Florence; and (e) the long range results of the period.

13. Why was Italy called the "School of Europe"? Explain the influence of Italy in four specific developments. Describe and discuss Machiavelli, his chief ideas, his chief works, and explain how he was a "typical" product of his times.

14. Explain the specific nature of the monarchy, nobility, clergy, towns, and serfs and how they influenced France, England, Spain, Germany, Milan, Florence, and Venice in the period.

15. Comment: In the late Middle Ages, older forms and attitudes became rigid and sterile.

16. Comment: The economic leaders of Italian cities made their impact not only on politics but also on the whole "style" of the age.

Period Roundup: The Medieval World

1. Compare and contrast the four civilizations (Western
   Europe, Byzantium, Russia, and Islam) that faced each
   other around the thirteenth century. Discuss geography,
   economy, social structure, government and law, religion
   and the Church, culture (including fine art, architecture, literature, science and technology, and philosophy), and general spirit and style.

2. Consult the chart on the next page, and compare and
   contrast two other civilizations or periods in the
   items given.

3. Compare and contrast Eastern, Western, and Russian
   Christianity. Discuss differences in dogma and tehol-
   ogy, monasticism, church organization, ritual, church
   architecture, relationship between church and state,
   and the role of the Church and religion in life.

4. Compare and contrast the Italian city states of the late
   Middle Ages with the Greek city states.

5. Compare and contrast the role of government in Western
   Europe in the early Middle Ages (800-1300) and the late
   Middle Ages (1300-1500).

6. Explain Roman Catholic theology in the medieval period
   under these headings: (a) nature and attributes of God;
   (b) nature of Man; (c) place of the Church; (d) sacraments; (e) Sin; (f) cults; and (g) popular religion.

7. Define the term "feudalism". Was it a "system"?
   Describe the sources of feudalism. Describe its
   supposed purposes, its organization in theory and in
   fact, and discuss the factors which prevented it from
   accomplishment of its purposes.

8. Describe the rights and duties of lord and vassal in
   feudalism.

9. Draw a map of a "typical" medieval man, label all of
   the parts, and describe how the manor was run.

10. Describe a day in the life of a "typical" serf.

11. Describe and discuss the organization of the medieval guild, the medieval fair, and medieval economic philosophy.

12. Describe the growth of the legal systems and the various kinds of courts and explain the system of justice used for the manor, the towns, the nobility, and the Church.

13. Describe the medieval cathedral and its place in the town and in the lives of the people.

14. Describe, discuss, and evaluate the medieval university and compare it with present universities in organization, faculty and administration, admission, student life, curriculum, method of instruction, requirements, and the obtaining of degrees. Explain the place of the university in the middle ages and its contribution to the modern universities.

15. Why has the medieval period been called the "Dark Ages"? To what extent is the term accurate? Describe the main cultural trends and achievements of the period.

16. What do we mean by the term "medieval synthesis"? Explain the economic, social, political, religious, and cultural facets of the whole synthesis.

Period Roundup: The Medieval World

2. See question #2 from previous page. If possible from
   material in the textbook and lectures, compare and contrast two areas or civilizations listed in <u>Group A</u> below with each other in several of the titems from the
   list in <u>Group B</u>. For example: England and France after
   1300 in geography, economy, social structure, government, religion, culture, and general spirit and style.
   The two lists, below, are very complete and of course
   comparisons of all items is hardly possible.

GROUP A

Western Europe to 1300
  Carolingian France
  France 987-1314
  England to 1066
  England 1066-1307
  Germany 911-1273
  Italy 911-1273
Byzantium to 1081
Kievan Russia
Islam to 1081
Western Europe 1300-1500
  France 1314-1483
  England 1307-1509
  Germany 1273-1515
  Italy 1300-1500
    Milan
    Venice
    Florence
  Spain to 1516
Byzantium 1081-1453
Ottoman Empire to 1699
Muscovite Russia

GROUP B

Geography and its influence

Economics, trade

Classes, social structure
  Nobility
  Towns
  Gentry and serfs
  Clergy
  Monasteries

Government
  Monarchy
  Nobility
  Representative bodies
  National administration
  Local administration
  Law, courts, justice

Religion, the Church
  Church and State
  Church and individual
  Theology

Culture
  Painting, sculpture
  Architecture
  Literature
  Science and technology
  Philosophy

General Spirit and Style

Chapter 11

The Renaissance

In studying the Renaissance, it is important to be aware of
the varied and distinct senses in which the term can be and
has been used: chronological, geographic, cultural, and
even political and economic. Chronologically, the Renaissance lasted for about three hundred years, extending from
the fourteenth through the sixteenth centuries. Since the
fourteenth and fifteenth centuries constitute the last two
centuries of the Middle Ages, and the sixteenth century is
normally considered the first century of "modern" times,
the Renaissance has correctly been called a period "neither
fully medieval nor fully modern, but a transition between
the two." Geographically, there were two Renaissances, for
in the fourteenth and fifteenth centuries Italy was the
home of the most important developments, while in the sixteenth century the center of activities shifted to northern
Europe. The era was also marked by an important and far-
reaching economic shift to a money economy which had a pro-
found impact upon both towns and manors and brought to the
forefront the rich merchants and bankers of this florid age.
The Renaissance was a political age featuring the new national
monarchies and their flamboyant rulers, rising independent
city states and their colorful business ruling class, and
the bombastic Renaissance popes with their equally elegant
Vatican court. Renaissance politics produced the political
morality of Machiavelli and a life style symbolized in the
book of etiquette written by Castiglione. While most
historians agree about the nature and significance of these
characteristics of the age, the term Renaissance was origi-
nally used and is most often understood to be a cultural
term. We now know that the Renaissance was not a "rebirth"
of interest in classical antiquity in the sense that the
term implies that the medieval period was indeed the "Dark
Ages" when ancient culture all but disappeared from western
Europe. Rather, the Renaissance saw the domination of
Humanism, which represented an obvious shift in emphasis from
the way the Scholastics of the High Middle Ages viewed the
classical heritage. Yet the Humanism of the Renaissance is
not easy to define clearly if we must present clear and
"typical" examples, for there are no such "typical" literary
or artistic figures whose works are entirely Renaissance
and show no kinship with the Middle Ages. We shall study
the leading authors to see to what extent their works are
"Renaissance" in character and yet how, at the same time,
they displayed medieval hallmarks. In a separate section, we

shall see that architecture, sculpture, and painting displayed
these same two distinctive dispositions.

The Renaissance was assuredly a magnificent period full of
monumental and flamboyant personalities who should stir the
interest and imagination of every human being. This was
an age when giants walked among us and tried to show how
life should be seen and felt and -- above all -- lived.

TOPIC OUTLINE

I. Introduction
   A. Renaissance defined
   B. Historical problem
      1. Location, time period, spread known
      2. Was it a "rebirth?"
      3. Various interpretations
         a. The new age -- Gibbon
         b. Burckhardt and Italian genius
         c. Heir of the medieval age

II. Rise of a Money Economy
   A. Terms defined
   B. Trade
      1. Baltic and the Hans
         a. Rise and growth
         b. Items and areas of trade
         c. Political, military, legal policies
         d. Decline -- causes
      2. Mediterranean towns
         a. Locations
         b. Items and methods of trade
         c. Venice as outstanding example
            Extent, items of its trade
            Policies -- Impact -- The galley
   C. Industry
      1. Leading examples
         a. Textiles
         b. Mining and metals
         c. Shipyards and arsenals -- Venice
      2. Impact on guild system
      3. Banking and Capital
         a. Role and need of banking in period
         b. Lombard bankers -- rise and decline
         c. House of Medici
         d. NonItalian banking
            Jacques Coeur Fuggers England

D. Town and countryside
   1. Population of some important towns
   2. Areas of heaviest interaction
   3. New roles for old classes
      a. Merchant role in countryside
      b. Nobility in towns, business role
      c. Serfs, rural workers, new roles
   4. Manors changed
      a. Examples, methods, results
      b. Serfdom decline peasant unrest
E. Political results of new economic trends
   1. Worker unrest and revolts
   2. Growing wealth differential -- results
   3. Influence of business class grows
      a. Direct rule of some towns
      b. Indirect role -- loans and trade
F. Impact on "style" of the age
   1. Shift in patronage of culture
   2. Personal pride and materialism
   3. Growing merger of business and noble classes

III. Literature and Thought
   A. Language and medieval values
      1. Latin for learning, "serious" thought
      2. Vernaculars for popular literature
         a. How spoken languages became "official"
         b. Regional dialects, predominance of one
         c. Romance, Germanic vernaculars
         d. Impact on nationalism
   B. Humanism
      1. Definitions
         a. Classical languages, studies, curriculum
         b. Literary style -- Cicero
      2. Classical values, ideas
         a. Scholastics use of the classics
         b. Renaissance use, growing secularism
      3. Humanists and the vernaculars
   C. Writers of the early Italian Renaissance
      1. Dante Alighieri (1265-1321)
         a. Medieval, Renaissance qualities
         b. Vernacular use -- practical politics
         c. Success during lifetime
      2. Petrarch (1304-1374)
         a. Family, training, career
         b. Classical, scholarly career
            Latin authors -- Letters to classical
               authors
            Mixing of old and new

                    Criticism of medieval, own day
          c. Vernacular poetry -- Sonnet form
          d. Success and fame
    3. Boccaccio (1313-1375)
          a. Education, business career, turn to
              classics
              vernacular use -- anticlericalism of
              sources, themes, tone -- example of plot
D. Later writers, scholars
    1. Classical Scholarship
          a. Humanistic enthusiasm for classics
          b. Search for ancient manuscripts
                  methods, places visited, authors found
                  Greek classics especially
          c. Libraries Patrons, uses of
          d. Greek scholars -- Manual Chysoloras
                  Platonic Academy in Florence
                  Barriers to full success
          e. Latin scholars
                  Examples of bad influences
                  Examples of good and bad influences
          f. Lorenzo Valla (1407-1457)
                  Character, career, nature of his work
                  Donation of Constantine
    2. Vernacular Writers
          a. Geoffrey Chaucer (1340-1400)
                  Medieval, Renaissance characteristics
                  Carrer, Italian travels and influences
                  Tone, examples of his Canterbury Tales
          b. Francois Rabelais (1494-1553)
                  Thorough Renaissance characteristics
                  Classical training -- career
                  Mastery of language, science
                  Abbey of Theleme, moto, way of life
    3. Philosophical Humanists
          a. General characteristics
          b. Marsilio Ficino and the Platonic Academy
                  Sources used, methods, aims
          c. Pico della Mirandola (1463-1494)
                  Education, tolerance of many values
                  and ages
                  Search for universal knowledge, truths
                  Unique position of Man in universe
          d. Erasmus (1466-1536)
                  Why call the "Prince of Humanists"
                  Career, travels, extent and nature his
                  works
                  Praise of Folly -- style, subject matter

                            136

                    Attributes of Renaissance Humanism
                    Influence on Protestant Revolution
IV. Science and Religion
    A. The Age of Preparation for later advances
       1. Humanists aid, hinder advancement
       2. Leonardo da Vinci (1452-1519) as example
          a. Inventiveness, insight, fine drawings
          b. Poor notes, no systematic methods
    B. Invention and technology
       1. Printing
          a. Advances in paper, printing from woodcuts
          b. Movable type in 1440s
          c. Examples of rapid and important results
       2. Gunpowder, artillery, firearms -- results
       3. Ships, navigation improvements
       4. Mining and metals -- Agricola
    C. Medicine
       1. Advances in anatomical illustrations, books
          a. University of Padua as center
          b. Vesalius, anatomy book
       2. Uncritical acceptance of Galen block progress
          a. Paracelsus, new drugs, rejects Galen
          b. Ambroise Pare and surgery
    D. Astronomy and Copernicus (1473-1543)
       1. Heliocentric universe theory
          a. Ptolemy, theory of spheres rejected
          b. Philosophical, religious implications
       2. Errors, limitations in Copernicus' theories
    E. Music
       1. Medieval Gregorian chant, plainsong
       2. New polyphonic, secular music
          a. New instruments, growth professional groups
          b. Palestrina and des Pres as leaders
          c. Patronage, music in court life
    F. The Renaissance and the Church
       1. Did it make Reformation inevitable?
          a. Individualism turn anti-clerical?
          b. Humanism turn anti-Christian?
          c. Materialism turn anti-Church?
       2. Strength, health of Church of time
          a. Shortcomings of priests, pishops, popes
          b. Powerful events test power
          c. Renaissance Popes
                Famous patrons of the arts, politicians
                Reform ignored
          d. Intellectual vitality of clergy lost?
                Blind defense of Scholasticism
                Reuchlin -- Letters of Obscure Men

                              137

3. Renewal and Reform
   a. Councils and the Papacy
   b. Spain, Queen Isabella, Cardinal Ximenes
   c. Brothers and Sisters of the Common Life
      Founding, aims, members, life
      Schools -- success of -- Eramus on
      Thomas a Kempis, Imitation of Christ
   d. Savonarola (died 1498) and moral puritan-
      ism
         Aims, methods, sample sermon
         Supporters -- political power, program
         Pope Alexander VI -- death

V. The Renaissance Way of Life
   A. Definition difficult
      1. Extraordinary yet different personalities
      2. No "typical" example in literature or the arts
   B. Special qualities identify all great figures, works
      1. Evidence of Castiglione's The Courtier (1528)
      2. Concept of the "Universal Man"

Chapter 12

The Protestant Reformation

Of all the important events in the history of the West, few more clearly illustrate the problems and dangers involved in historical investigation and interpretation than the Protestant Revolution. The topic had to be handled with both caution and detachment in high school, for it is frought with deep feelings and prejudices. But college students ought to be mature enough, as well as intelligent enough, to see in this even the real complexity of history, with its endless possibilities for new and interesting interpretations. After all, how many events have produced two such provocative theories as those of Weber and Erikson on single facets of the Protestant Revolution?

Students and professors who can bring a fair mind to this chapter, realizing their own prejudices as part of their intellectual baggage, may come away with rewards which go far beyond mere information about the events. We should all sense the deep and sincere personal conflict suffered by Martin Luther in his time of soul searching. In agreement with him or in opposition, we should feel for a troubled human being. In the same way, we should be able to appreciate the colossal greatness of some of the Renaissance popes -- especially Julius II -- as we try to understand why they could not apply their genius to religion as they did to the arts. We may begin to appreciate how a king cannot separate his public and private life when we see how Henry VIII shattered his private life because of his need for a male heir. Yet this simple dynastic problem led to a clash with the papacy and religious results which Henry certainly never wanted.

We shall see how young John Calvin came to differ with the logic of the Church and substituted a rigid system of logic of his own; how Zwingli could not feel near to his God in the splendor and ceremony of the Renaissance Church and so sought a simple and austere service and church; and how some people, feeling the need for a religious experience and expression which featured spontaneous, emotional enthusiasm, left the Church to become the Anabaptists. Finally, we shall see how the threat to "Mother Church," plus the spirit of the Renaissance and of movements from the Middle Ages, came to produce the Catholic Reformation. Controversy may surround the Inquisition and the Index, but the real dilemma may be the Jesuits, with their combination of enthusiasm, intellectualism, and pragmatism.

To understand any of these things well, we will have to enter the thought and feeling processes of the people involved -- while at the same time recognizing clearly our own predispositions -- and try to understand their problems and solutions in the European scene of their own day, not the world we live in.

TOPIC OUTLINE

I. Introduction
   A. How Reformation was touched off
   B. Was it a "reformation" or a "revolt?"
   C. Breakdown of medieval religious unity
      1. Earlier reform movements
      2. Decline of papacy -- conciliar movement
      3. Renaissance and medieval value system
   D. Original aims, final results of Luther's act

II. Protestant Founders: Martin Luther
   A. Luther's spiritual crisis
      1. Family, early life, education
      2. Turn to monastic life
         a. Search for values, own salvation
         b. Bible study
      3. Faith -- answer to his problems?
   B. Attack on Indulgences
      1. Indulgences in theory and practice
         a. Tetzel's indulgences -- granted, or sold?
         b. Ninety-five theses
      2. Gradual broadening of attack
         a. Attack of other Catholic practices
         b. Criticism of pope
         c. Questioning, rejection of "good works"
         d. Priesthood of all men
   C. Defiance of Papacy and the Empire
      1. Cardinal Cajetan -- Leipzig debate with Eck
      2. Appeal To the Christian Nobility
         a. Authority of pope, church councils rejected
         b. Preisthood of all men
      3. Final break -- Ban by Emperor
         a. Papal Bull burned -- excommunication
         b. Diet of Worms of 1521
         c. Emperor Charles V's action
      4. Defiance, victory for Luther
         a. Protection by the princes
         b. National popularity
         c. Translation of the Bible into German
   D. Reasons for Luther's success

1. Wordliness of the Church -- corrupt practices
2. German nationalism -- Luther's Bible, hymns
3. Economic factors -- Princes' role
4. Luther's personality
5. Attractiveness of his ideas -- justification by faith alone
6. Weakness of forces against him
    a. Leo X -- failure of reform, compromise
    b. Emperor Charles V's decision to fight
    c. Charles V, Ferdinand and Germany
    d. Religious Wars (1521-1555)
    e. Peace of Augsburg (1555)
        Terms -- religious meaning
        Political terms -- property issue
E. Luther: a conservative revolutionary
    1. Possible implications his philosophy
        a. Nature his Saxon church, clergy
        b. Nature his social, economic views
    2. Princely conversion to Lutheranism
        a. Economic, social, political motives
        b. Reaction of other classes
    3. Knights' War (1522) and Peasants' Rebellion
        a. Grievances -- types involved -- demands
        b. Luther's response to Twelve Articles
    4. Luther turns to established churches, princes

        b. Conservative views consistent?
    5. Results
        a. Gradual conversion of Germany, Scandanavia
        b. Loss of initiative to others

III. Zwingli, Calvin, and Other Founders
    A. Zwingli
        1. Humanist training -- Location, time his reforms
        2. Fundamental beliefs -- General philosophy
            a. Clergy, service, church building
            b. Community discipline, righteous living
            c. Opposition to Catholic "superstition"
                View of Eucharist
                Compared with transubstantiation, consubstant
                Compared with Catholic, Lutheran view
            d. Zwingli compared with Luther in doctrines
        3. Influences on Protestanism
    B. Calvin
        1. Family, legal training, spiritual crisis
        2. Personality -- compared with Luther
        3. Basic ideas: Institutes of the Christian Religion

                a. Break with Catholic ritual, organization
                b. Logical completeness, vigor
            4. Response, spread of his ideas
                a. Geneva, the City of God, the "Protestant
                    Rome"
                b. Scotland, Germany, other areas
                c. France the Huguenots
                    Response of King Francis I
                    Beginning of long religious wars
    C. The English Reformation and Henry VIII
            1. Henry VIII's clash with the pope
                a. Marriage problem -- annulment request
                b. Causes refusal of annulment -- result
                c. Henry's annulment and excommunication
                d. Act of Supremacy (1534) Terms; results
            2. Antipapal, anticlerical tradition in England
            3. Henry, the monasteries, the middle class
            4. The Anglican Church -- What was it?
                a. Catholic dogma, ritual; no pope, monasteries
                b. Opposition
                        Catholics -- More, Fisher -- defeat
                        Protestants -- Six Articles -- Cause,
                            terms
            5. General results
                a. Gradual Protestantization of Anglican
                    Church
                b. England center of religious variation (sects)
    D. Anabaptists and Other Radicals
            1. Anabaptists
                a. Basic philosophy, practices
                    Adult baptism -- source of name "Anabaptists"
                    Return to "true church" of early times
                    Private Bible interpretation
                    Social reform -- own communities
                    Menno Simons -- Anabaptist way of life
                b. John of Leiden, extremists at Munster
                        Social rules -- community -- antinomian-
                        ism
                c. Persecution of -- how they survived
                d. Present day groups derived from them
            2. Mysticism and Unitarianism
                A. Schwenkfeld -- individual inner spirit
                        Opposition to formal religion
                        present location -- persecution of
                b. Unitarians -- Servetus, Socinus
                        Basic philosophy -- mysticism in
                        Compared with modern Unitarians
                        Location of groups -- persecution

IV. Protestant Beliefs and Practices
    A. Common denominators
       1. Reject Catholic claim as only "true faith"
       2. Own claims as "true faith"
          a. Persecution in period -- religious toleration
          b. Separation of church and state in period
       3. Reduction in ritual, church organization
          a. Monasteries, clerical celibacy ended
          b. Sacraments reduced -- disputes over
          c. Church buildings, services, practices changed
       4. Rebels seek return to "purity" of early church
       5. Appeal for justification to "higher law"
       6. Individual judgment -- individualism
    B. Conservative Churches
       1. The Church of England (Anglican, Episcopal)
          a. Range of possible beliefs and practices
                High Church and Low Church
                Puritans -- Erastianism
          b. Thirty-Nine Articles (1571) as compromise
                Catholic practices rejected
                Stand on hierarchy, clergy, Eucharist
                Reject priesthood of all, Faith alone
       2. Lutheran
          a. Strong Erastian trend
          b. Conservative elements -- influence of
                Luther
                Hierarchy, services, music
                Eucharist
          c. Strong evangelical party -- future influence
       3. Calvinism
          a. Basic dilemma: free will vs. predestination
                Problem explained -- some earlier answers
                Calvin's logic -- The elect, the damned
          b. Calvinism in practice
                Puritanism, ethical persuasion, sermons
                Influences on other sects
                Arminian opposition
          c. Theocracy, not Erastianism -- Moral "force"
    C. The Protestant Radicals
       1. Calvin's influence
       2. Wide variation in practices
          a. Wild extremes -- Munster -- not the rule
          b. Enthusiasm in services, preaching
          c. Often reject oaths, state -- Pacificists
          d. Chiliastic (2nd coming, end of the world)
          e. Pious, communal living -- equality

3. Alarmed others -- harsh persecution
4. Later groups (Baptists, Quakers, Mennonites)

V. The Catholic Reformation
   A. Background
      1. Nature of Catholic Reformation
        a. Negative defense, suppression?
        b. Rally of spiritual and material forces?
      2. Source of Protestant ferment: within the Church
        a. Widespread spiritual crisis -- Humanism
        b. Some left Church -- Other remained
   B. Elements of the Catholic Reformation
      1. Aid of Catholic Rulers -- Examples
      2. New orders of the regular clergy
        a. Oratory of Divine Love -- Theatines
        b. Capuchin branch of Franciscans
        c. Ursuline nuns
        d. The Jesuits
            Loyola -- life -- turn to religion
            Aims, rules -- <u>Spiritual Exercises</u>
            Criticism of Jesuits
            Work, record, successes
      3. The Inquisition
        a. Medieval use by papacy, Spain -- methods
        b. Use against Protestants -- methods
        c. Protestant tradition about
      4. The Council of Trent
        a. Role of pope Paul III -- groups called
        b. Work, accomplishments
            No compromise of doctrine -- role of
               clergy
            Reform of practices -- uniformity out-
               lined
            The <u>Index</u> -- purposes, methods
      5. Reforming Popes -- Pius V as example
   C. Results of Catholic Reformation
      1. Doctrinal definition, practices reformed
      2. Spread of Protestanism stopped

VI. Conclusions
   A. Protestantism, Progress, and the Modern World
      1. Progress of northwestern (Protestant) Europe
        a. Democracy, science, technology, culture
        b. Was Protestantism the cause?
        c. Examination of "truth of the myth"
      2. Fundament agreement of Catholics and Protestants
        a. Progress, better life in future?
        b. Religious toleration?

    c. Separation of church and state?
    d. Social equality? Mass political partici-
        pation?
  3. Role in challenge of old authority
B. The Weber Thesis
  1. Protestantism and capitalist success
  2. Calvinism: hard work, "simple" living
    a. Production, consumption results
    b. Business success and the "elect"
  3. Evidence to support, refute the thesis
C. The Reformation and Nationalism
  1. Usual mixture: religion and patriotism
  2. Notable exceptions

MAP EXERCISE Map No. 12, The Protestant Revolution

Locate   the countries of Norway, Sweden, Russia, Prussia,
          Poland, Saxony, Moravia, Denmark, Scotland, Ireland,
          England, the Netherlands, France, Wurtemberg, Austria,
          Bohemia, Switzerland, Hungary, the Ottoman Empire,
          Portugal, Spain, Italy, and the Holy Roman Empire.

Locate   the cities of Erfurt, Augsburg, Leipzig, Wittenberg,
          Zurich, Basel, Bern, Geneva, Munster, Wurtemberg,
          Trent, and Rome.

Locate   the areas of the religious situation of about 1600
          and show the locations of the Roman Catholics,
          Lutherans, Zwinglists, Calvinists, Anabaptists,
          Anglicans, and the Orthodox Churches and Islam

PEOPLE, TERMS, EVENTS

Martin Luther   Ulrich Zwingli
Tetzel   John Calvin
indulgences   Institutes of the Christian
John Eck   Religion
To the Christian Nobility   Huguenots
Justification by Faith   Henry VII and Catherine of Aragon
good works   Act of Supremacy
transubstantiation   The Thirty-Nine Articles
consubstantiation   Anglican Church
Diet of Worms   Erastianism
Peace of Augsburg (1555)   Sir Thomas More
Peasants' Rebellion (1524-1525)   Theocracy
Knights' War (1522)   Arminiamism

145

Anabaptists
John of Leiden
Munster Anabaptists
Menno Simons
Casper von Schwenkfeld
Unitarians
Servetus
Fausto Sozzini
Socinians
predestination
Free Will
John Bunyan, Pilgrim's Progress
mysticism
Protestant ethic

pietism
Oratory of Divine Love
Theatines
Capuchins
Ursuline nuns
Ignatius Loyola
The Spiritual Exercises
Jesuits (Society of Jesus)
Pope Paul III
Council of Trent
Index
Inquisition
Weber Thesis

SAMPLE QUESTIONS

1. Describe the long-range and general causes of the Protestant Revolution. Consider previous reformers and
   critics, Church practices, the papacy, church councils,
   the sacramental system, theology, philosophical causes,
   some psychological problems, and social, econoimc, and
   political causes.

2. Describe the immediate causes in German social, economic,
   and political conditions. Mention the role of nationalism in relations between Germany the papacy. Describe
   the philosophical, theological, and psychological
   problems faced by Martin Luther.

3. Describe the ideas of justification by faith alone, the
   priesthood of all true believers, and Luther's ideas
   about the common people and the state and show the
   logical problems in his ideas and how he resolved them.

4. Describe the general and specific objections of Calvin to
   Catholic doctrines and practices. Describe his alter-
   native doctrines and practices.

5. Do the same for Zwingli.

6. Do the same for the Anabaptists. How did the social and
   economic background of the Anabaptists come to be
   reflected in their philosophy and practices.

7. Describe the political problems faced by Henry VIII of
   England concerning his marriage. Why did this lead to

a break with the Church? What events and movements in the English tradition made a subsequent move towards Protestantism inevitable? Discuss the idea that the revolution in England was more social and economic in its results than religious.

8. Describe and discuss the Weber thesis of the connection between Protestantism and Capitalism. Why does Calvinism fit the thesis best?

9. Discuss the thesis that the protest and revolt of Martin Luther was more personal and psychological, an identity crisis, than it was based on general philosophical and religious principles.

10. Describe the long-range causes and the immediate causes of the Catholic Reformation.

11. Would there have been a Catholic Reformation with or without the Protestant Revolution? Would the nature of the Catholic Reformation have been the same or different?

12. Why was Spain the chief leader of the Catholic Reformation? Describe the role of the papacy, the Jesuits, the Inquisition, and the Index.

13. Was a Reformation needed? Was a Revolution necessary to get it?

14. Why did the various Protestant churches and the Roman Catholic Church fail to get together and work out a compromise?

15. Why did all the groups in the period practice persecution?

16. Describe and discuss the impact of the Protestant Revolution upon individualism, democracy, religious freedom and toleration, and capitalism.

147

Chapter 13

Dynastic Politics and Warfare, 1494-1648

Developments in politics during the sixteenth century, along with the cultural contributions to the Northern Renaissance made by the Spanish, French, and English, are treated in this chapter. Comparable to what we saw in the last chapter in religion, political developments that had their beginnings in the late Middle Ages now became recognizable as modern. The competitive state-system of sovereign and independent states, with war as their final arbiter of rivalries and disputes, became characteristic of European politics and diplomacy. Only the development and refinement of national diplomacy, particularly the technique of maintaining the balance of power, kept the resulting international anarchy within bounds and preserved a modicum of order within the state-system.

The modern character of these developments is underlined by the fact that even in our own day the diplomacy of the balance of power has remained the chief practical hope for the preservation of world peace.

The wars of the sixteenth century, as well as the Thirty Years' War of the early seventeenth century, were the products of dynastic rivalry and religious intolerance. Yet political factors played a large part in the so-called wars of religion, and the rivalry of the Valois-Bourbon and Hapsburg dynasties also included larger question of whether the European state-system would be replaced by another empire on the Roman model.

Within the sovereign states of Western Europe, determined kings took advantage of a demand for security and order to establish themselves as absolute monarchs and usher in the "Age of Absolutism." In particular, Spain, building upon the foundations laid by Ferdinand and Isabella at the end of the fifteenth century, became the wealthiest and most powerful absolute monarchy, and the predominance and then decline of Spain runs as the most important thread through the history of the sixteenth century and the first half of the seventeenth. We shall also observe the rise of England to a powerful position and the brief but spectacular success of the Dutch Republic and the kingdom of Sweden.

TOPIC OUTLINE

I. Introduction: The Balance of Power
   A. Watershed date: medieval to modern?
   B. Rise of the competitive state system
      1. Meaning of term "sovereign"
      2. States, wars, sovereignty in the middle ages
      3. "Scorecard lineup" of emerging states
      4. Threats to these states, system, since 1400
      5. How status quo preserved -- main thread since
   C. Nature of political units (1494)
      1. Distinction between dynastic and nation state
         a. Examples, characteristics of dynastic state
         b. Dynastic state in war -- peace settlements
         c. Mixed nature of some states -- examples
         d. Danger of overemphasis of change
      2. Instruments of foreign policy

II. Hapsburg, Valois, Tudor, and Orange
   A. The Italian Wars of Charles VIII and Louis XII
      1. Charles's invasion of Italy (1494)
         a. His reign in France, features of
         b. Pretext, real reasons for invasion
         c. Holy League against -- significance -- defeat
      2. Louis XII's invasion
         a. Claims in Italy -- failure diplomatic intri-
            gue
         b. New Holy Alliance -- his defeat
   B. Charles V (Hapsburg) versus Francis I (Valois)
      1. First phase (1525-1535)
         a. Possession of Charles V -- France in a vice
         b. Defeat, capture of Francis I at Pavia (1525)
         c. Effect of "rules" of warfare of time
         d. Sack of Rome (1527) by army of Charles V
         e. Crowning of Charles by pope -- meaning
      2. Second phase (1535-1559)
         a. Francis gains allies
         b. Role of England -- Protestants
      3. Peace settlements (1555-1559)
         a. Peace of Augsburg (1555) with Protestants
         b. Peace of Chateau-Cambresis (1559) with French
   C. The Wars of Philip II (1556-1598)
      1. Possessions of Philip after division of empire
      2. His personality, aims
      3. His five major areas of involvement
         a. Italy, France, Mediterranean, New World
         b. Netherlands

            Traditional autonomy -- His policy changes
            Points of disagreement
    4. The Dutch Revolt (1566-1609)
       a. Duke of Alba policies -- results
       b. North and south split -- causes -- results
       c. Duke of Parma -- policies -- results
       d. North independent -- South remains Hapsburg
       e. Factors in Dutch victory -- role of England
    5. Last years of Philip
       a. Conquest of Portugal (1560)
       b. Battle of Lepanto (1571) -- significance
       c. Spanish Armada (1588) -- significance
    6. Evaluation

III. The Catholic Monarchies: Spain and France
  A. General Characteristics
    1. Age of Absolutism, Divine Right Monarchy?
       a. Meaning and validity of terms
       b. Centralization, uniformity
    2. Role of local nobility, local way of life
  B. Spanish Absolutism
    1. Charles V (Charles I of Spain)
       a. Attitude towards, rule of Spain
       b. Revolt of <u>comuneros</u> -- causes and results
    2. Philip II
       a. Centralization, use of councils, own role
       b. The nobility, clergy, cortes
       c. Finances and taxes -- Limits on income
       d. Nature and results of regionalism
       e. Evaluation his role in Spanish greatness
    4. The Spanish economy
       a. Resources, potential and real wealth
       b. How strength and wealth lost
           War, inefficiency, unsound mercantilism
           Low domestic production, foreign smug-
             gling
           Spanish life style and character
    5. The Spanish style
       a. General characteristics
       b. How different from other Latin cultures
       c. Examples in literature, painting, religion
  C. France: the last Valois kings
    1. France under Francis I (advantages, weaknesses)
       a. His Renaissance traits and habits
       b. Local privileges, the nobility, the estates
       c. The Church, the Concordate of Bologna (1516)
    2. Wars of Religion (1562-1598)
       a. Weak successors to Francis I

        b. Classes and districts of Huguenot strength
        c. Nobility and monarchy -- polarization
        d. Charles IX and Catherine de Medici
                St. Bartholomew's Day massacre
                Foreign intervention -- causes, results
        e. War of the Three Henrys (1585-1589)
                Personalities -- Revolts, plots, murders
                Triumph of Henry of Navarre (henry IV)
    3. The First Bourbon: Henry IV
        a. Foreign intervention (Spain) defeated
        b. Religious settlement
                Henry's conversion -- political realism
                Edict of Nantes (1598) -- terms of
    4. The politiques role (Jean Bodin)
        a. Religious toleration, for unity
        b. Political unity, centralism, law and order
    5. Henry IV as popular king and hero
        a. Personality, wit, realism
        b. Economic aims, policies
        c. Fiscal weakness as heritage of policies

IV. The Protestant States
    A. England
        1. Henry VIII (1509-1547)
            a. Life style, wars, sound finances
            b. New rich nobility, new poor
            c. Henry and parliament -- Makeup, powers
            d. Administration by the "ruling elite"
        2. Edward VI and Mary (1547-1558)
            a. Edward VI and the move to Protestantism
            b. Mary and Catholic restoration
        3. Elizabeth I (1558-1603)
            a. Religious settlement and problems
            b. Personality and Renaissance traits
            c. Mary Stuart -- Catholics -- conspiracy
            d. War with Spain -- Armada
            e. Parliament grows restless and resistive
            f. The Irish Question
        4. The English Renaissance
            a. Causes
                    Prosperity, success, religious unity
                    Good leaders, administration
            b. Upper class joining in arts, patronage
            c. Literature is glory of period
                    Examples -- Characteristics
    B. The Dutch Republic
        1. Greatness, size, leadership in period
        2. Economic position, policies

            a. Shipping, fisheries
            b. Banking and insurance
            c. New industry -- Progress in agriculture
        3. Government
            a. Traditional strong local home rule of pro-
                vinces
            b. Estates General -- stadholder
        4. Religion: policies and influences
            a. Toleration, freedom, refugees
            b. Growth of publishing, universities
        5. The Dutch Style in Greatness

V. Germany and the Thirty Years' War (1618-1648)
    A. Nature and causes of the war
        1. Political
            a. Hapsburg threats to balance of power
            b. Emperor vs. German princes
        2. Religious
            a. Calvinists and the Peace of Augsburg
            b. Protestant Union vs. Catholic League
    B. Bohemian period (1618-1625)
        1. Czech revolt -- Ferdinand II crushes
        2. Involvement of others -- Palatinate and Spain
    C. Intervention by Denmark and Sweden (1625-1635)
        1. Catholics and Spain near victory
        2. Denmark (Christian IV) comes to aid Lutherans
            a. Catholic League, Wallenstein, victory over
            b. Harsh settlement -- resultant threat
        3. Sweden (Gustavus Adolphus) enters war
            a. Alliance with France (Richelieu) -- terms
            b. Protestants hesitate -- Sack of Magdeburg
            c. Swedish victories -- death of Gustavus
            d. Wallenstein abandoned, assassinated
            e. Growing Hapsburg, Catholic victories
    D. The Hapsburg-Bourbon Conflict (1635-1648)
        1. Changed nature of war, aims
            a. Religious concessions granted
            b. Professional armies in Germany
        2. French, Dutch victories over Spain
        3. Long conference for peace -- issues of
    E. The Peace of Westphalia (1648)
        1. Religious terms -- end of religious wars
            a. Ecclesiastical reservations
            b. Multiplicity of sects -- minority rights
        2. Territorial terms
            a. Gains for France, Sweden, Brandenburg
            b. Sovereign rights for German states

  c. Independence of Swiss Confederation and
    United Netherlands recognized
 F. Results of the war
  1. Immediate results on Germany
   a. Economic, population, morale effects
   b. Continuation of bitterness
  2. Terrible nature, extent of war -- effects
  3. Long-range effects more serious?

MAP EXERCISE

Locate these bodies of water: Baltic Sea, North Sea, Atlantic Ocean, Mediterranean Sea, Adriatic Sea, Aegean Sea,
   and Black sea.

Locate these cities: London, Copenhagen, Stockholm, Paris,
   Nantes, Amsterdam, Leyden, Antwerp, Metz, Verdun, Toul,
   Magdenburg, Augsburg, Berlin, Prague, Vienna, Genoa,
   Milan, Venice, Florence, Rome, and Madrid.

Locate these areas: Norway, Sweden, Denmark, Russia, Lit-
   huania, Poland, Ukraine, Khanate of the Crimea (1550),
   Ottoman Empire, Holy Roman Empire, Prussia, Brandemberg,
   Pomerania (1648), Silesia, Saxony, Bohemia, Moravia,
   Austria, Hungary, Tyrol, Bavaria, Wurttemberg, Bavaria,
   Switzerland, Burgundy (1550), Alsace (1648), Franche
   Comte (1648), Luxembourg, Netherlands (1550), United
   Netherlands (1648), Spanish Netherlands (1648),
   Westphalia, Palatinate, France, Avignon, Savoy,
   Piedmont (1648), Milan, Genoa, Corsica, Tuscany,
   Venetian Republic, Ionian Islands, Crete, Cyprus, Papal
   States, Sardinia, Sicily, Naples, Portugal, Spain,
   Balearic Islands, Ireland, Scotland, and England.

TERMS, PEOPLE, EVENTS

sovereignty	hidalgo
state-system	gentry
balance of power	Irish question
Dynastic state	Huguenots
Nation state	politiques
cortes	Elizabethian settlement

Puritans
Brownists
stadholder
Utraquism
Casa de Contratacion
ecclesiastical reservation
Francis I
Charles VIII
Catherine de' Medici
Coligny

Louis XII
Henry III
Henry of Navarre
Henry IV
Edict of Nantes
John Bodin
Battle of Pavia (1525)
St. Bartholomew's Day Massacre
Treaty of Vervins
Concordate of Bologna (1516)

Charles V
Treaty of Cateau-Cambresis
Emperor Ferdinand II
Defenestration of Prague
Cardinal Richelieu
Gustavus Adolphus
Sack of Magdeburg (1631)
Peace of WEstphalia
Cuius regio eius religio
Catholic League
Philip II
Duke of Parma
The "Beggars"
Comuneros revolt (1520)
Cervantes
Spanish Armada (1588)

Sack of Rome
Emperor Ferdinand I
Czech Revolt of 1618
Christian IV of Denmark
Wallenstein
Edict of Restitution (1629)
Count Tilly
Thirty Years' War
Protestant Union
Battle of Lepanto
Duke of Alba
Council of Blood
William the Silent
St. John of the Cross
Don Quixote

Henry VIII
Edward VI
Mary Stuart (Queen of Scots)
Anne Boleyn

Six Articles
Mary I (Tudor)
Elizabeth I
Lady Jane Grey

SAMPLE QUESTIONS

1. Explain the difference between a dynastic monarchy and
    a nation state, with many examples.

2. Show how Charles V was more of a dynastic monarch and how
    Philip II tried to be king of a nation state.

3. Compare and contrast the personality, aims, and methods
    of Charles V and Philip II. Evaluate each.

4. Make a case for and against the idea that Charles V,
    Philip II, Francis I, Henry IV of France, Henry VIII,

154

and Elizabeth I were "great" rulers.

5. Compare and contrast the Spanish, Dutch, and English "style."

6. Describe and discuss the religious problem in England and the course of development under Henry VIII, Edward VI, Mary Tudor, and Elizabeth I.

7. Describe, discuss, and evaluate the causes and nature of Dutch greatness in the period. Why did it fail to last?

8. Describe, discuss, and evaluate the causes and nature of Spanish predominance in the period. Describe the economy, social structure, government, religion, and culture of Spain in the period. What were her weaknesses? Could her greatness have lasted?

9. Describe and discuss the causes and nature of the Dutch Revolt. Why was Philip II unable to deal with the problem? What were the results of the revolt?

10. Describe and discuss the idea of the balance of power in theory and in practice. Why did the state system which grew up in this period have to have and use the balance of power? What might have happened otherwise?

11. Describe and discuss the causes of the Thirty Years' War in Germany, both religious and political.

12. Explain how the Thirty Years' War changed from a "local" war in Germany to an international war.

13. Explain how the religious issues of the Thirty Years' War declined in importance and how some countries were involved directly or indirectly in the war on a side not in accord with their own religious connection.

14. Describe, discuss, and evaluate the terms of the Peace of Westphalia on Western Europe in general; on Germany.

15. What were the immediate results of the Thirty Years' War on Germany? The long-range results?

16. To what extent are the terms "Age of Absolutism" and "Divine Right Monarchy" accurate for this period?

17. Describe the development of national and local government in England under the Tudors. Explain the relations of the Tudor monarchs with their parliaments. Did the composition of the parliament have anything to do with these good relations?

18. Describe, discuss, and evaluate the development of England from a minor power to a great power in the period.

19. Describe, discuss, and evaluate the distinctive features of the English Renaissance, with many examples.

Chapter 14

The Expansion of Europe to Early Modern Times

The Expansion of Europe describes a "geographic renaissance"
that led to numerous voyages of discovery and culminated in
European domination of much of the world by the end of the
seventeenth century. This expansion resulted from a complex
variation of factors, perhaps most of them coming from the
developments of the Renaissance.

The Renaissance spirit of inquiry was certainly responsible
for the original desire to know more about the rest of the
world and its peoples and each new discovery only added a few
facts on which more and more speculation could be made about
what might be discovered in the future. Furthermore, most of
the people we read about in this chapter were little different
from the writers and artists of the Renaissance and the fact
that we now study their exploits will fulfill their wildest
dreams of fame and glory.

We should also mention that the Protestant Revolution and the
Catholic Reformation had an impact upon both exploration,
especially by Catholic missionaries, and of settlement of
many parts of North America by groups who were refugees from
the Catastrophe of the Thirty Years' War in Germany and of
religious conflict elsewhere.

While these psychological and spiritaul motives can be ignored
only if one wants an incomplete picture, there were other
motives in the expansion of Europe.

The absolute monarchs of western Europe often exercised
arbitrary controls in an effort to make themselves and their
states more powerful. Just as for reasons of power they sought
to control the Church within their borders, so for similar
reasons they thought it even more essential to control the
economy of their states. This policy of state regulation of
economic life is called mercantilism. Wealth was seen as the
basis of power, and a favorable balance of trade, with more
wealth entering than leaving the state, was the goal set by
these monarchs. Trade in Oriental goods, not only costly in
themselves but made more so by passing through various middle-
men on the long route between the Indies and western Europe,
was the area of trade in which an extremely unfavorable
balance caused most concern. To circumvent this, the Portugese first succeeded in finding a far cheaper route to India,
and so Lisbon replaced Venice as the depot for Oriental goods

in the West. Chiefly through the voyages of Columbus and
Magellan, Spain quickly established its own routes to the
New World and to the Orient by sailing westward. Then the
English, French, and Dutch were looking for routes of their
own. Thus began the first great age of European economic
imperialism. Commercial capitalism, already flourishing
under the leadership of Italian and German merchants, now
greatly expanded from the new centers bordering the Atlantic.
During the sixteenth century, Portugal and Spain were the
great commercial and imperial powers, but they were destined
to be replaced in the first half of the seventeenth century
by the Dutch. In the last half of that century, the English
and French began to push the Dutch aside and to embark on a
long rivalry for world empire that continued into the last
half of the eighteenth century.

TOPIC OUTLINE

  I. Introduction
      A. Exploration and expansion, old and new
          1. Greek, Roman, Chinese
          2. New features after 1492
              a. Speed -- distance -- oceans
              b. Contact with other cultures and peoples
              c. Western physical superiority
              d. Spiritual, psychological motivation?
          3. Technology and the scientific spirit
          4. Search for trade routes
      B. Earlier European voyages -- Vikings -- Fishing

 II. East by sea to the Indies
      A. Portugese exploration
          1. Prince Henry the Navigator
          2. Motives for Portugese exploration
          3. Around Africa to India -- Dias -- da Gama
          4. Treaty of Tordesillas (1494)
          5. Cabral and South America (1500)
          6. Trading practices -- regulation -- China
      B. The New World outside Europe
          1. Africa
              a. Black empires, cultures
              b. Africa and Europe -- impact on each other
          2. India
              a. Earlier contacts -- new contacts
              b. How Europeans dominated
                      Military superiority
                      Indian disunity -- Rivalry of rulers

European impact on India, China compared
   c. Indian civilization and life
      Geographic variations -- Aryan invasion
      Caste -- meaning and influence
      Hindu religion -- Buddhism -- influences
  3. China
   a. Features earliest civilization
      Contacts with Europeans, others
      Manchu conquest, civilization
   b. Elements of change
   c. Elements of continuity
      village -- mandarins -- emperor
   d. Religion -- Confucianism -- upper class role
C. The Portugese Empire
  1. Nature of the empire -- trade
  2. Policies and practices
   a. Economic -- mercantilism
   b. Military
   c. Colonial -- relations with the natives
      Europeanization and the masses
      Christianization -- missionaries
  3. Causes of decline
   a. Internal weaknesses -- external pressures
   b. Empire after decline

III. West by Sea to the Indies
  A. Columbus and later explorers
    1. Columbus (1451-1506)
      a. Spain -- motives in aid -- his commission
      b. His own motives, concept of earth
      c. Four voyages -- results
    2. Naming the new continent -- Amerigo Vespucci
    3. Later Explorers
      a. Ponce de Leon and Florida (1512)
      b. Balboa, Panama and the Pacific (1513)
      c. Others in Latin America
      d. Northwest Passage search
      e. Southwest Passage -- Magellan (1519-1522)
  B. The Spanish Colonial Empire
    1. Role of the conquistadores
      a. Cortes, Pizarro, others
      b. Pre-Columbian empires -- their greatness
      c. Fate of these empires
    2. Nature of the Spanish empire
      a. Racial composition of population
      b. Geographic separation of units -- results
      c. Administration
         Centralization, paternalism, mercantilism

                    Growth of local influence and voice
            d. Economy of Spanish America
                    Production and trade -- items
                    Labor problem -- <u>encomienda</u> -- slavery
        3. Evaluation of Spanish record
            a. Treatment of the Indians
            b. Missionaries and Catholicism
        4. Comparison: Portugese and Spanish colonies

IV. The North Atlantic Powers and Russia
     A. English, Dutch, and Swedes in North America
         1. Early explorations -- Cabots
         2. English interloping on Spain -- Drake
         3. The English colonies
             a. Raleigh and the Roanoke colony (1584)
             b. Jamestown and Plymouth
             c. Dutch and Swedish colonies -- loss of
             d. The Thirteen Colonies
                     Social, religious background of settlers
                     Geographic influences
                     North-South differences as result
             e. Myth and fact about early colonies
                     religious toleration -- democracy
                     Comparison with Spanish, Portugese
                         colonies
     B. New France
         1. Exploration -- Cartier, Champlain
         2. Westward push -- geographic advantage
             a. Missionary zeal -- fur trade
             b. Mercantilism, direction from France
         3. Geographic extent of New France
             a. Character of the empire
             b. Weaknesses of the empire
     C. The Indies, West and East
         1. Caribbean -- Spanish hold broken
             a. English, Dutch, French holdings
             b. Economy and importance
         2. India
             a. Defeat of Portugese, position checked
             b. French and English holdings, rivalry
             c. Nature of holdings -- role in politics
         3. Dutch in Southeast Asia
     D. Africa and the Far East
         1. Africa -- importance on sea route
             a. Costal holdings -- Dutch settlement
             b. Interior untouched and unexplored
         2. Far East
             a. China -- stations there -- missionaries

                            160

b. Japan -- trading rights -- missionaries
c. Attitudes China, Japan towards Europeans
E. East by Land to the Pacific
1. Russian exploration and Expansion in Siberia
a. Ural mountains (1483) -- role of monarchy
b. Pacific reached (1644) -- Cossack role
Fur trade -- Church -- administration
Compared with American advance to the
Pacific
2. Contact with Chinese -- Treaty of Nerchinsk
(1689)
F. North by Sea to the Arctic
1. English, Hudson Bay -- Hudson's Bay Company
2. Dutch, Barents Sea, Spitsbergen
3. Russia, Siberian coast, Bering Sea

V. The Impact of Expansion
A. The Human and Economic Record
1. Bad side of record
a. African slave trade -- racism
b. Fate of native populations
c. Mercantilism and natural resources
2. Good side -- mostly came later
B. Effects of Expansion of the West
1. New items in life-style
2. Broadening of mental horizons
3. Cultural interchange
4. Material progress
a. Inflation and economic expansion
b. Social change
c. Webb's "frontier thesis"
C. Toward One World
1. International politics and war
2. World trade

MAP EXERCISE Map No. 14, The Expansion of Europe

Locate   these bodies of water and rivers: the Atlantic,
Pacific, Indian, and Arctic Oceans; the Barents,
Bearing, and Caribbean Seas; Hudson Bay and the Bay of
Fundy; the Indus, Ganges, Yellow, Yangtze, Amur, St.
Laurence, Hudson, Mississippi, Orionoco, Amazon, La
Plata, and Gambia rivers.

Locate   in Europe the United Netherlands, England, France,
Sweden, Norway, Spain, Portugal, Italy, the Ottoman
Empire, Russia, the Ural Mountains, and the cities of

161

London, Lisbon, Cadiz, Madrid, Seville, Genoa, and
Venice; the Azores, Madira, Canary Islands, and the
Cape Verde Islands, and Spitsbergen.

Locate____ in North America the Bahamas, the West Indies, Cuba,
Santo Domingo, and the Isthmus of Panama; Greenland,
Iceland, Newfoundland, the Grand Banks, New France,
Massachusetts Bay Colony, Delaware, Virginia, Florida,
and Roanoke Island; and the cities of Plymouth, Quebec,
New Amsterdam, Jamestown, Fort Christiana, and New
Orleans.

Locate____ in Latin America New Granada, Guiana, Peru, Mexico,
Venezuela, Brazil, Bolivia, Chile, Paraguay, and the
locations of the Inca and Aztec empires.

Locate____ in Africa the Gold Coast, Senegal, Guinea, the Cape
of Good Hope, Madagascar and the Mali and Ghana empires
and the city of Timbuktu.

Locate____ in Asia the Mogul Empire (of India), India, Ceylon,
China, Japan, Manchuria, Mongolia, Siberia, Formosa,
the Philippine Islands, Dutch East Indies, New Zealand,
New Holland, Java, Sumatra; the cities of Goa, Surat,
Calicut, Madras, Calcutta, Nagasaki, Peking, Macao,
and Canton.

Locate____ the line of the Treaty of Tordesillas, Magellan's
voyage, and the possessions of Portugal, Spain,
England, the Dutch, and France in 1715.

TERMS, PEOPLE, EVENTS

Vikings
Prince Henry the Navigator
Marco Polo
Vasco da Gama
Treaty of Tordesillas
Aryan
Brahmin
nirvana
Mahayana
Zen Buddhism
mandarin
trading "factory"
Ferdinand and Isabella
Amerigo Vespucci

Vasco Balboa
Ferdinand Magellan
Francisco Pizarro
Inca empire
Creoles
audiencia
Council of the Indies
John Cabot
Jacques Cartier
John Hawkins
Humphrey Gilbert
Roanoke colony
Mogul Empire
Treaty of Nerchinsky

162

Leif Ericson
Preston John
Bartholomeu Dias
Pedro Cabral
Alfonso de Albuquerque
caste
Gutama Buddha
Hinduism
Hinayana
Manchu Dynasty
Confucianism
mercantilism
Christopher Columbus
Ponce de Leon

Northwest Passage
Hernando Cortes
Aztec empire
encomienda
mestizos
cabildo abiertos
Bartolome de las Casas
Giovanni de Verrazzano
Henry Hudson
Francis Drake
Sir Walter Raleigh
East India Company
St. Francis Xavier
Webb's "frontier thesis"

SAMPLE QUESTIONS

1. Describe and discuss the differences between expansion in the ancient world and in the 1492-1715 period.

2. Describe, discuss, and evaluate the major causes of the 1492-1715 period of exploration and expansion. Mention economic, political, scientific, psychological, spiritual, and other causes.

3. To what extent did the Renaissance play a role in the exploration and expansion?

4. Describe, discuss, and evaluate the role of the Protestant Revolution, the Catholic Reformation, the religious wars, and other religious motives and events.

5. Why was Europe successful in expansion against the peoples and states of Asia, Africa, and the Americas?

6. Why were China and Japan best able to resist?

7. Why did the Chinese and Japanese regard Europeans as inferior?

8. Why was only the coast of Africa explored and not the interior?

9. Describe the various voyages of discovery in chronological order.

10. Describe the colonial system of the Portugese, Spanish, English, and French. Describe their economic, social, political, and religious policies and practices.

11. Define mercantilism in theory and show how policies of Spain and England were adopted to achieve the objectives of the system. Give specific policies and acts.

12. Describe treatment of the native population of the colonial empires of the Portugese, Spanish, Dutch, French, and English.

13. Describe the social and economic results of the expansion of Europe and of imperialism upon Europe itself.

14. Describe the results upon the rest of the world.

15. Why did the states of central and southern Europe not join in the search for colonies and trading empires?

Chapter 15

Divine-Right Monarchy -- and Revolution

The first half of the seventeenth -entury saw the culmination
of the long rise of absolute monarchy in western European
politics. Buttressed in the period by an appeal to religion
in the form of the theory of divine-right by the Frenchman,
Bishop Bossuet, and by an appeal to reason by means of the
social convenant theory of Thomas Hobbes, absolutism reached
its zenith. It is fitting that France, home of Bossuet and of
Louis XIV, the greatest exponent of the divine-right theory,
should replace Spain in this century as the predominate power
of Europe. The results of the Thirty Years' War indicated
this fact, but the reign of Louis XIV made it clear to every-
one. The reign of Louis XIV threatened the security of much
of Europe, but the balance of power was restored by the time
of his death. However, there was no decline in the leadership
and prestige of French cultural leadership to parallel her
loss of political and military domination.

While divine-right did reach the height of its acceptability
in the seventeenth century, a new trend in politics also
became firmly established. Opposition to absolute monarchy,
which we have seen in the Dutch revolt against the Spanish
Hapsburgs, now appeared on a larger and more significant
scale in England. There, a revolution against the Stuart
dynasty was able to produce only the dictatorship of Cromwell.
But a second effort, the Glorious Revolution of 1688, perma-
nently forestalled English absolutism. There followed the
first victor of what we call representative or parliamentary
government, which became the model for political reform in
the future. This model was given its philosophical framework
by the Englishman John Locke, whose political theories
became the basis of the American Declaration of Independence
and many other calls for liberty and representative government.

This chapter also deals with the "Century of Genius" in
science, thought, literature, and music. The culture of
this century, and its continuation into the eighteenth
century, is called "classical" because of it spirit of having
found perfection and truth in certain "scientific" forms
and techniques, in the discovery of universal "laws" that
explained the operation of the universe. Inspired by the
scientific discoveries of the period, the rationalists of
these two centuries carried over the search for universal
truth into every field of human interest, believing that
human reason can discover and apply Natural Law in everything.

In so doing, they declared their break with the doubt of the previous century and from the values of the medieval synthesis. At the same time, they predicted a rosy future of perfection if these Natural Laws were only discovered and applied.

TOPIC OUTLINE

I. Introduction
    A. End of an epoch (symptoms of)
    B. Beginning of a new era
        1. The French Century
            a. Louis XIV and Divine-Right Monarchy
            b. French danger to balance of power
            c. Le grande nation -- French style, culture
        2. English Revolutions
        3. The century of genius
        4. The age of many crises

II. Bourbon France
    A. Louis XIII and Richelieu
        1. Louis XIII, Marie de' Medici, Estates General
        2. Richelieu as chief minister
            a. Principles, methods (Raison d'etat)
            b. Huguenots
            c. Foreign policy -- armed forces
            d. Centralization of power
            e. Defects of his system
        3. Mazarin as successor, imitator of Richelieu
            a. Childhood of Louis XIV
            b. Alienation of nobility
            c. Fronde (1648-1653)
            d. Comparison with Richelieu
    B. Louis XIV, Le Grande Monarque
        1. Personality, character, health, life style
        2. Versailles -- the palace -- the symbol
        3. Divine-Right Monarchy
            a. Theory -- Reasons idea accepted
            b. Practice -- Reasons not realized
        4. Obstacles to absolutism
            a. Nobility -- fate elsewhere -- types
                Louis' use of -- opposition
            b. The Church and the clergy
                Declaration of Gallican Liberties (1682)
                Corporate privileges of Church, clergy
                Quietism -- Jansenism

166

                c. Huguenots
                        restriction and then coercion
                        revocation of Edict of Nantes (1685)
                        Huguenot fate -- influence elsewhere
        5. Royal Administration under Louis XIV
                a. King, his ministers, departments of state
                b. Intendants in <u>generalite</u> -- <u>subdelegues</u>
                c. Local administration: independence of
        6. Mercantilism: Theory of economic absolutism
                a. Domestic aims and methods
                b. Foreign, colonial aims and methods
        7. Mercantilism in practice -- Colbert system
                a. New industry -- fate of manor, guild
                b. Trade regulation -- overseas trading compa-
                        nies
                c. Internal transportation -- roads, canals
                d. Economic leadership gained, lost
C. French Expansion under Louis XIV
        1. Goals (3 possible) of territorial expansion
                a. Louis XIV's use of each
                b. Cultural imperialism
        2. Instruments of imperialism
                a. Ministry of Foreign Affairs
                b. Army reforms -- failures of -- leadership
        3. First wars and early success
                a. War of Devolution (1667-1668)
                        causes, aims, results
                b. Dutch War (1672-1678)
                        causes -- Triple Alliance against France
                        role of William of Orange -- of England
                        Treaty of Nimwegen (1679) -- terms
                c. French power, prestige at peak by 1679
        4. Failure in last two wars
                a. War of the League of Augsburg (1688-1697)
                        Causes -- members of the League
                        Role of England -- seapower influence
                        Peace of Ryswick (1697) -- terms, results
                b. War of the Spanish Succession (1701-1713)
                        Causes -- members of Grand Alliance
                        Course of war in Europe, North America
                c. Peace of Utrecht (1713) -- Landmark treaty
                        General principles
                        European, American settlements and terms
                        Defects, future problems as result
        5. French Aggression in Review
                a. Horrors of battle, home front problems
                b. Religion as an issue
                c. Case of "classical" aggression?

III. Stuart England
    A. Background
        1. England and continent compared in government
            a. Machinery of absolutism
            b. Constitution, law, consensus, tradition
            c. Role of nobility, gentry
        2. Stuarts and Tudors compared
            a. Personality
            b. Political philosophy
            c. Attitude towards Parliament -- handling of
        3. Crown and Parliament
            a. Composition of the Parliament -- classes
            b. Issues between
                Finances, religion, foreign affairs
    B. The reign of James I (1603-1625)
        1. Traditional issues magnified
            a. Finances, taxes
                The king, the Parliament, the courts
                Parliamentary grants or royal preroga-
                    tives?
            b. Foreign affairs
                Royal marriage -- king or parliament?
                Great Protestation (1621) -- dissolution
            c. Religion
                Elizabethian settlement -- fate under
                    James
                Hampton Court Conference failure
        2. Culture: the King James Version of the <u>Bible</u>
    C. The difficulties of Charles I (1625-1642)
        1. Wars, financial needs
            a. Parliamentary opposition
            b. Petition of Right (1628) -- 5 rights claimed
            c. Conciliation, more demands, firmness and
               arrests
        2. Period of personal rule (1619-1640)
            a. Taxation methods -- ship money
            b. Religious policies -- Archbishop Laud
            c. Economic plight of gentry; fact or fiction?
        3. Scottish rebellion, the Short Parliament
        4. Second rebellion, the Long Parliament
            a. Why called, powers position, reforms passed
            b. Attempt to arrest parliamentary leaders
            c. Parliamentary aims: Nineteen Propositions
               (1642)
    D. The Civil War (1642-1648)
        1. England divided -- Cavaliers vs. Puritans
            a. Royalist strength
            b. Parliamentary strength

2. Early royalists success
3. New Model Army -- Cromwell -- Charles defeated
   a. Moderates vs. radicals as result
   b. Religious, political issues
   c. Pride's Purge -- Rump Parliament
   d. Execution of Charles I (1649)
E. Cromwell and the Interregnum (1649-1660)
   1. The Commonwealth -- political organization of
      a. Radical, army domination
      b. Cromwell as dictator -- personality, aims
   2. Foreign affiirs
      a. Scottish revolt, Charles II
      b. Navigation Act of 1651, Dutch War
      c. Irish revolt; land "settlement"
      d. War with Spain -- Jamaica (1655)
   3. Cromwell and his parliaments
      a. Reform of Rump Parliament fails -- result
      b. The Protectorate
         Constitution: The Instrument of Govern-
            ment
         Election, modifications
         Military government -- Puritan virtue
         Cromwell death (1658) -- son Richard
            rule
   4. The Restoration -- Charles II
F. The Revolution in Review
   1. Reign of Terror and Virtue? -- The blue laws
   2. Victory over absolutism, arbitrary rule
      a. Parliament and control of finances
      b. Freedom of Speech -- Milton's Areopagitica
      c. Radical thought, the trend of the future
         Economic, social, political radicalism
         Levellers, Diggers
      d. Religious toleration -- Independents,
         Quakers
G. The Restoration (1660-1688)
   1. Charles II
      a. Religious settlement -- dissenters
      b. Puritan ways abandoned
      c. Foreign policy -- French alliance
         Dutch defeat -- New Amsterdam
   2. James II
      a. Declaration
      b. Catholic "danger" -- Declaration of Indul-
         gence
      b. Fear of absolutism -- bloody assizes, army
   3. The Glorious Revolution

H. The Glorious Revolution and Its Aftermath, 1688-1714
   1. Whig coup d'etat removes James II
      a. Birth of Catholic heir
      b. William III (William of Orange) and Mary II
      c. William of Orange invasion -- James flees
   2. William III and Mary II (1689-1702)
      a. Bill of Rights accepted (1689)
         Importance of, provisions
      b. Future steps (3) to parliamentary democracy
   3. The reign of Anne (1702-1714)
      a. Stuarts, the Old Pretender
      b. Act of Settlement (1701) and house of Hanover
      c. Union of England and Scotland (1707)
      d. Ireland -- religious and economic persecution

IV. The Century of Genius
    A. The Scientific Revolution
       1. Francis Bacon and the scneitific method
          a. Observation of nature, accumulation of data
          b. Inductive reasoning
       2. Aids in scientific advancement
          a. New instruments
                telescope, miscroscope, barometer, ther-
                   mometer
          b. Scientific socieites
                Royal Society and Academie des Sciences
                Official experiments, publication of
                   articles
                private correspondence of members
                international scientific community growth
          c. Mathematics development
                Decimals, logarithms, analytical geometry
                Game theory, the calculus, actuary tables
       3. Scientific discoveries
          a. Astronomy
                Kepler, Galileo on planet motion
                Galileo on falling bodies, pendulums
                Newton on motion, gravity, optics, color
          b. Geology -- Gilbert, earth as magnet
          c. Physiology
                Harvey on heart as pump
                Borelli on muscles, mechanics of body
                   movement
    B. The Implications of the new science
       1. Comparison of Aristotle and Galileo
       2. Newton's world-machine
          a. As scientific theory -- mechanistic world
          b. Theological, philosophical implications

        c. Rationalism and role of God
     3. Descartes, Discourse on Method
        a. View of authority
        b. I think, therefore I am
        c. God, world, Cartesian dualism
  C. Progress -- and Pessimism
     1. Idea of natural law, human reason
        a. Tradition of idea in history
        b. Idea of Progress added
            Human reason finds natural law
            application brings perfection
     2. Dispute over progress and perfectibility
        a. Hobbes, Leviathan (1651)
            Sinful nature of Man, chaos is result
            Liberty surrendered to government
        b. Locke, Second Treatise of Government (1690)
            Rational man, government convenient
            Right of revolution
     3. Continuation of Christian tradition
        a. St. Vincent de Paul (1581-1660)
        b. Blaise Pascal (1623-1662) as many sided
           genius
            Mathematics, physics, practical inven-
              tions
            Jansenist, mystic -- Pansees on Reason
        c. Baruch Spinoza (1632-1677) and pantheism
  D. The Classical Spirit in Literature
     1. Characteristics of Classical style
        a. Paris salon of Marquise de Rambouillet
        b. Dictionary of the Academy -- Boileau the
           critic
        c. Propriety, dignity, discipline, refinement
     2. French drama -- Corneille and Racine
  E. Baroque Music
     1. Characteristics of the style
     2. Frescobaldi, Monteverdi, the star system
     3. Purcell in England -- Lully in France

MAP EXERCISE Map No. 15, Divine-Right Monarchy and Revolution

Locate   the Atlantic Ocean, the North Sea, the Baltic Sea,
    and the Mediterranean Sea.

Locate   the chief independent countries after 1713: norway,
    Sweden, Denmark, the United Netherlands, Austrian Nether-
    lands, the Holy Roman Empire, Brandenburg, Prussia,
    Bavaria, Switzerland, the Palatinate, Spain, Portugal,
    and France.

Locate   Ireland, Ulster, Scotland, England, Sicily, Corsica,
         Sardinia, Savoy, Naples, Milan, Minorca, Gibralter,
         Franche Comte, and Alsace. (Districts, areas)

Locate   the Austrian Hapsburg holdings, the Holy Roman
         Empire, the Venetian Republic, and the Ottoman Empire.

Locate   the cities of Paris, Versailles, Nantes, La Rochelle,
         Milan, Naples, Utrecht, Rywick, Nimwegen, Augsbrug,
         and London.

Locate   the battles of Cape La Hogue, Roussillon, Blenheim,
         Malplaquet, Marston Moor, Naseby, Preston, and
         Worcester.

TERMS, PEOPLE, EVENTS

Louis XIII	Academy Dictionary
Marie de' Medici	Corneille
Mazarin	Raison d'etat
Fronde	Bishop Bousset
Parlement of Paris	James I
French Academy	Charles I
Louis XIV	Charles II
Richelieu	James II
Divine-Right	"No bishop, no king"
Gallican Church	Long Parliament
Quietism	Rump Parliament
Jansenists	Pride's Purge
Colbert	Puritans
mercantilism	Puritanism
Revocation of the Edict of Nantes	
War of the League of Augsburg	Ship money
War of the Spanish Succession	Archbishop Laud
War of Devolution	Court of Star Chamber
Peace of the Pyrenees	Instrument of Government
Triple Alliance	Francis Bacon
William of Orange	Galileo
Treaty of Nimwegen	Royal Society
Peace of Ryswick	Academic des Sciences
Prince Eugene of Savoy	Robert Boyle
Treaty of Utrecht	Kepler
asiento	Harvey
St. Vincent de Paul	Rationalism
Blaise Pascal	Newton
Pensees	Principia Mathematica
Baruch Spinoza	John Locke

Great Protestation (1621)
Grand Remonstrance (1641)
Hampton Court Conference
Thomas Wentworth, Earl of
    Strafford
English Reign of Terror and
    Virture
John Churchill, Duke of
    Marlborough
Rounhead, Cavalier
Oliver Cromwell
New Model Army
The Commonwealth
Navigation Act of 1651
The Protectorate
Blue laws
John Milton, <u>Areopagitica</u>
Levellers

Quakers
Independents
dissenters
nonconformists
Glorious Revolution
Declaration of Indulgence
Act of Settlement
William III and Mary
Bill of Rights (1689)
Rene Descartes
<u>Discourse on Method</u>
<u>I think, therefore I am</u>
Newtonian world-machine
Thomas Hobbes
<u>Leviathan</u>
<u>Second Treatise on Government</u>
Diggers

Period Roundup: 1300 - 1715

1. Evaluate the theory that there was a clear connection between the Renaissance and the Reformation.

2. Describe, discuss, and evaluate the causes, events, and results of the series of wars between 1494 and 1648, including the French wars in Italy, the wars between Charles V and Francis I, the wars of Philip II, and the Thirty Years War.

3. Describe, discuss, and evaluate the characteristics of Tudor government and administration, both national and local, and their relations with the Parliament.

4. Compare and contrast the causes (economic, social, political, and religious) of the Dutch and English revolutions.

5. Describe, discuss, and evaluate the rise and decline of Spain, Portugal, and France.

6. Describe, discuss, and evaluate the causes and results of overseas exploration and expansion.

7. Describe, discuss, and evaluate the chief theories in support of divine right monarchy.

8. Describe and sicuss divine right monarchy in theory and practice.

9. Describe and discuss mercantilism in theory and practice.

10. Compare and contrast the role of the monarchy, the nobility, and the middle class in England and France.

CHRONOLOGICAL CHART 1: 4000 B.C. to 300 A.D.

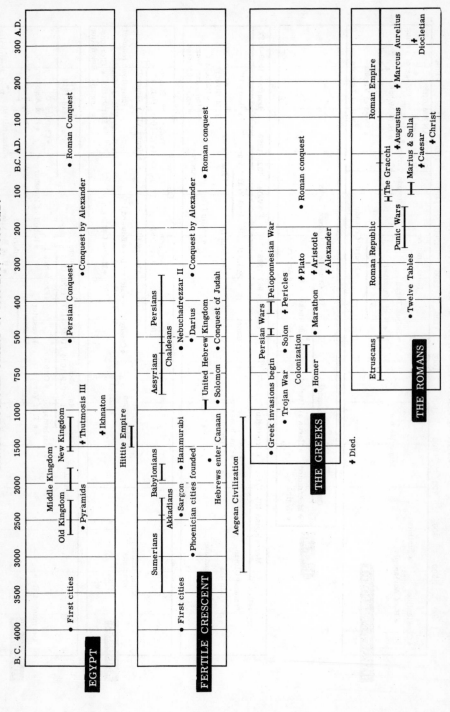

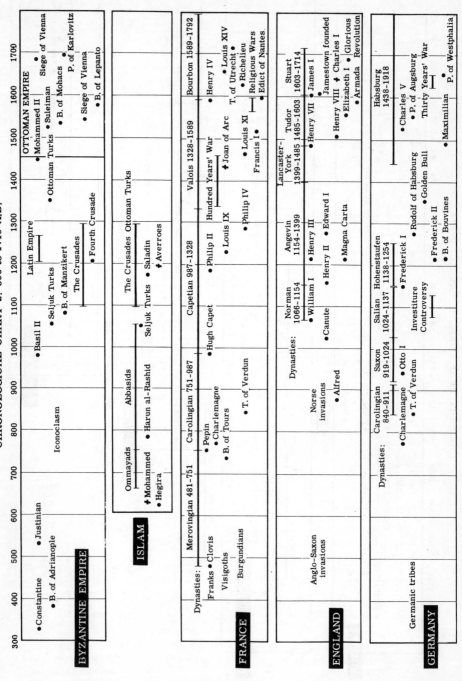

CHRONOLOGICAL CHART 2: 300 to 1715 A.D.

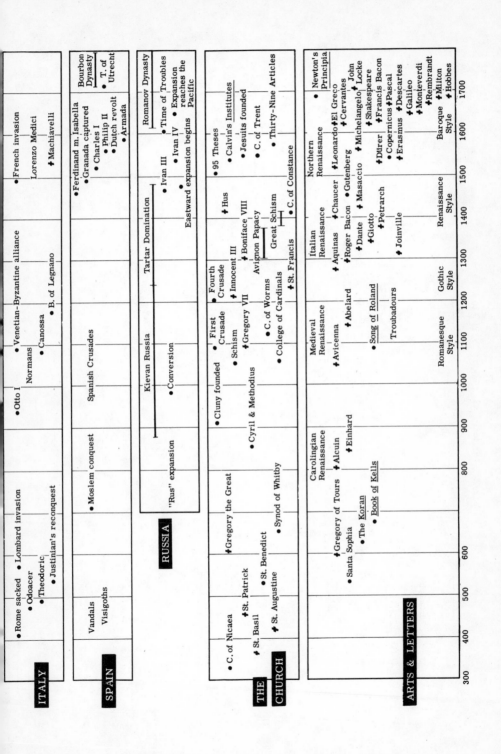

ITALY

- Rome sacked • Lombard invasion • Otto I • Venetian-Byzantine alliance • French invasion
- • Odoacer — Normans — Lorenzo Medici
- • Theodoric • Canossa • Machiavelli
- • Justinian's reconquest • B. of Legnano

SPAIN

- Vandals • Moslem conquest • Ferdinand m. Isabella — Bourbon Dynasty
- Visigoths • Granada captured • T. of Utrecht
- Spanish Crusades • Charles I
- • Philip II
- • Dutch revolt
- • Armada

RUSSIA

- Kievan Russia — Tartar Domination — Romanov Dynasty
- "Rus" expansion • Conversion • Ivan III • Time of Troubles
- • Ivan IV • Expansion reaches the Pacific
- Eastward expansion begins

THE CHURCH

- • C. of Nicaea ✝Gregory the Great • Cluny founded • First Crusade • Fourth Crusade • 95 Theses
- ✝St. Basil ✝St. Patrick • Schism • Innocent III • Calvin's Institutes
- • St. Benedict ✝Gregory VII ✝Boniface VIII ✝Hus • Jesuits founded
- ✝St. Augustine • Cyril & Methodius • C. of Worms Avignon Papacy • C. of Trent
- • Synod of Whitby • College of Cardinals Great Schism • Thirty-Nine Articles
- • St. Francis — C. of Constance

ARTS & LETTERS

- Carolingian Renaissance Medieval Renaissance Italian Renaissance Northern Renaissance • Newton's Principia
- • Santa Sophia ✝Gregory of Tours ✝Alcuin • Avicenna ✝Aquinas ✝Chaucer ✝Leonardo✝El Greco ✝John Locke
- • The Koran ✝Einhard • Abelard ✝Roger Bacon ✝Gutenberg ✝Cervantes
- • Book of Kells • Dante ✝Masaccio ✝Michelangelo ✝Shakespeare
- • Song of Roland • Giotto ✝Dürer ✝Francis Bacon
- Troubadours ✝Petrarch • Copernicus ✝Pascal
- • Joinville ✝Erasmus ✝Descartes
- ✝Galileo
- ✝Monteverdi
- ✝Rembrandt
- Romanesque Style Gothic Style Renaissance Style Baroque Style ✝Milton
- ✝Hobbes

300   400   500   600   700   800   900   1000   1100   1200   1300   1400   1500   1600   1700

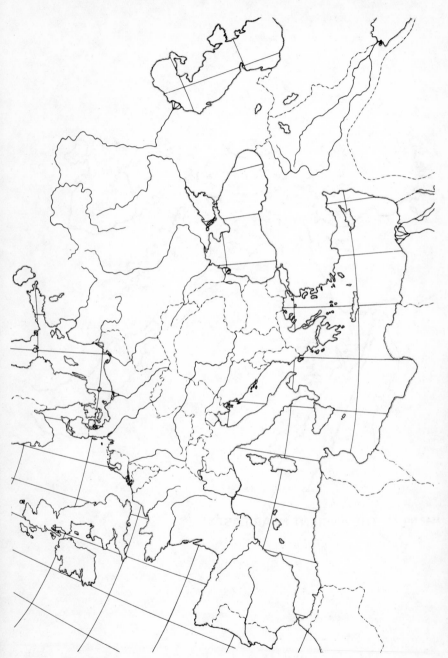

MAP NO. 1   EUROPE AND THE NEAR EAST IN 1939

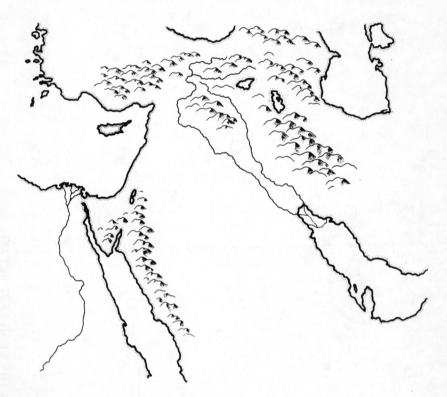

MAP NO. 2 THE ANCIENT NEAR EAST

MAP NO. 3   THE ANCIENT GREEK WORLD

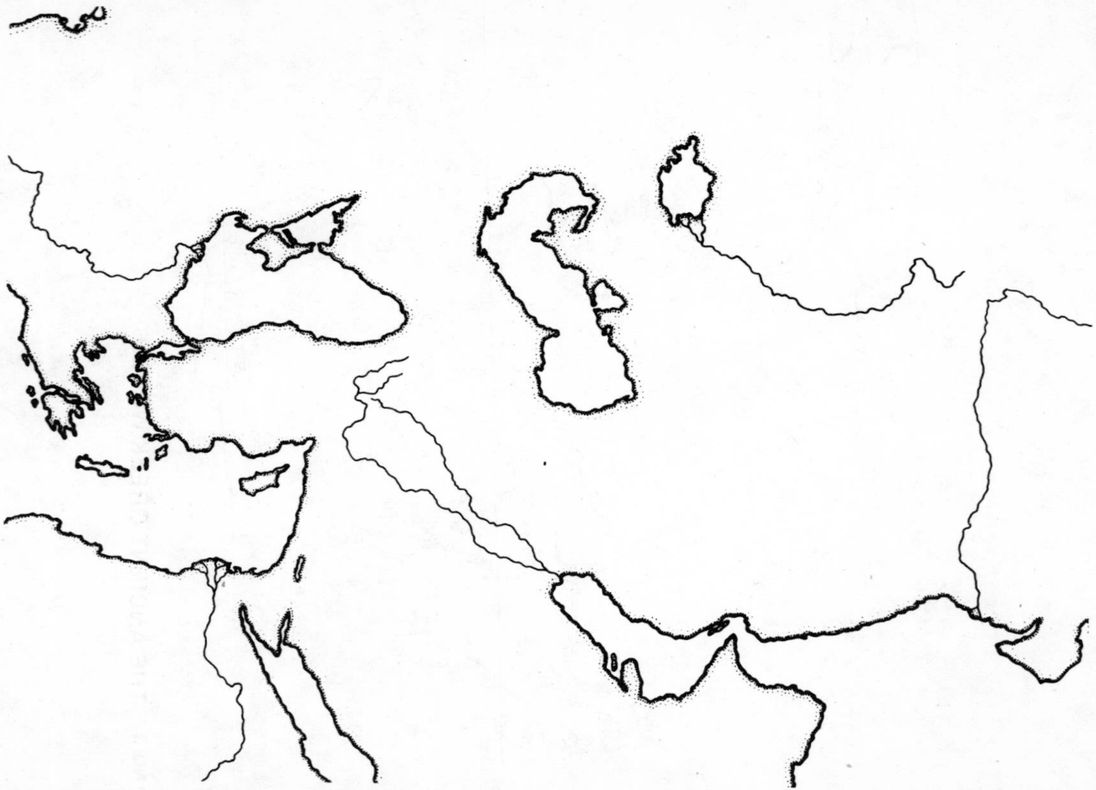

MAP NO. 4 ALEXANDER'S EMPIRE

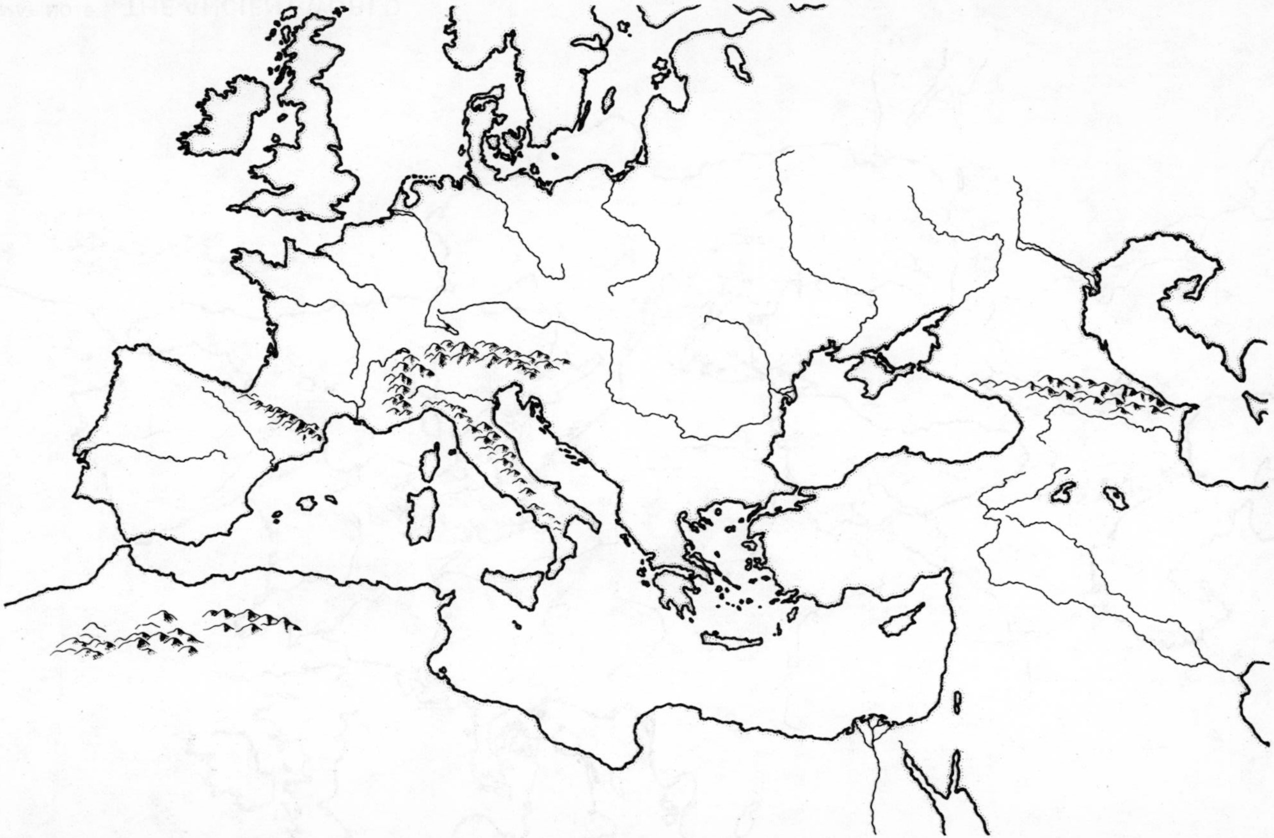

MAP NO. 5 **THE ROMAN WORLD**

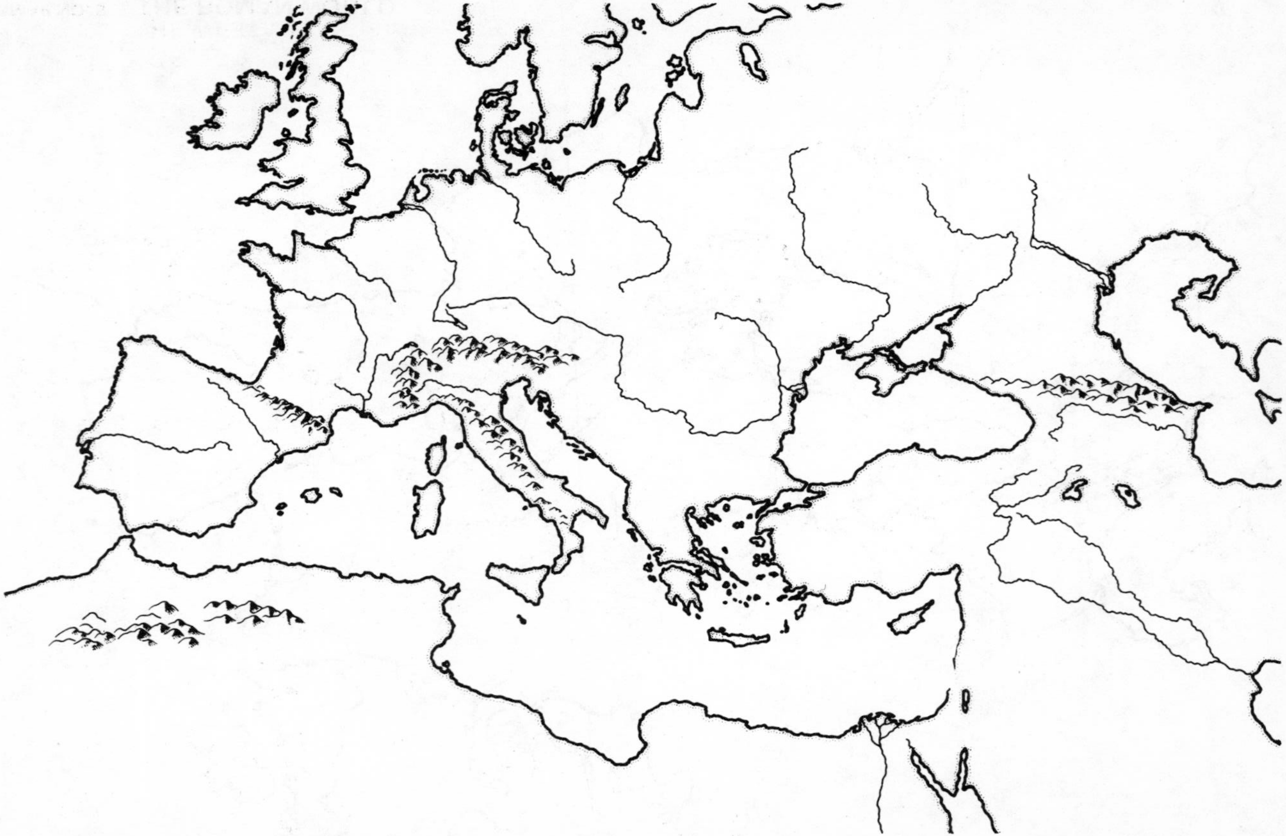

MAP NO. 6 THE ANCIENT WORLD

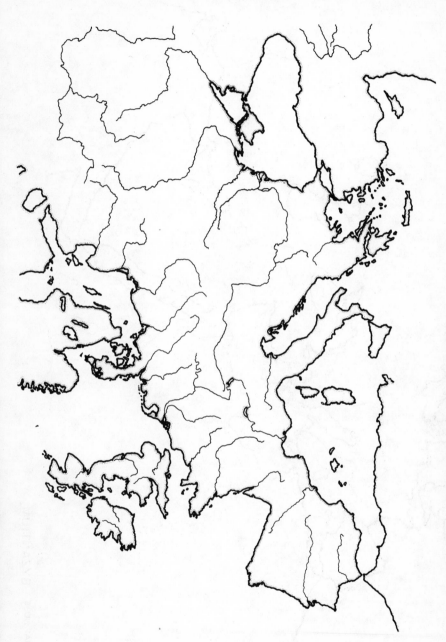

MAP NO. 7   THE WEST IN THE EARLY MIDDLE AGES

MAP NO. 8   BYZANTIUM

MAP NO. 9   THE SPREAD OF ISLAM

MAP NO. 10   THE EAST IN THE LATE MIDDLE AGES

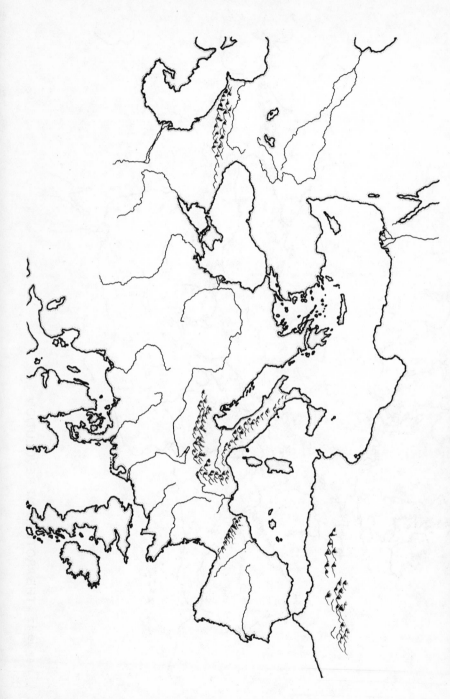

MAP NO. 11   THE WEST IN THE LATE MIDDLE AGES

MAP NO. 12   THE PROTESTANT REVOLUTION

MAP NO. 13   DYNASTIC AND RELIGIOUS WARS

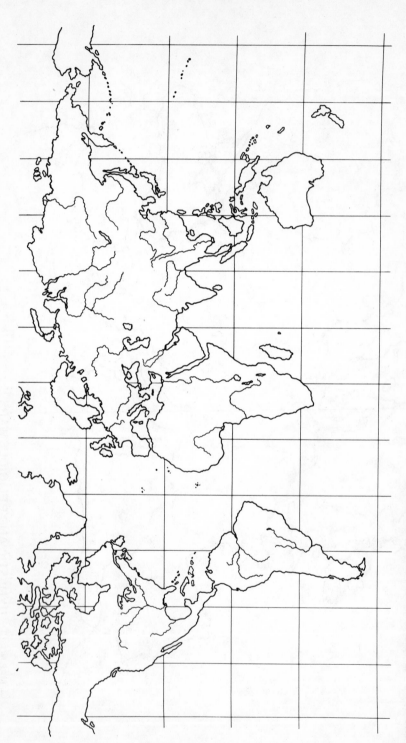

MAP NO. 14   THE EXPANSION OF EUROPE

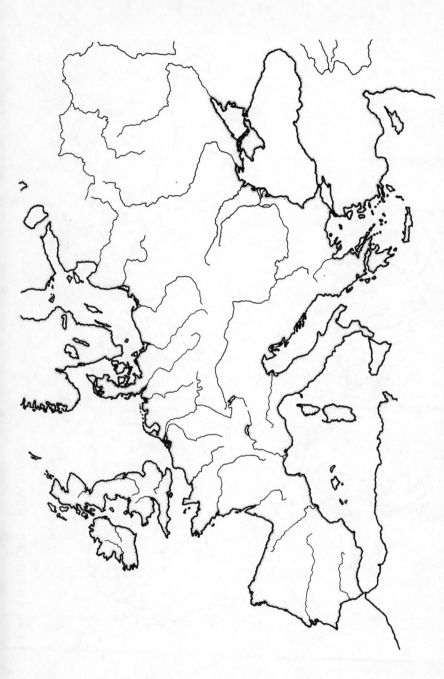

MAP NO. 15   DIVINE–RIGHT MONARCHY AND REVOLUTION

MAP NO. 16 EUROPE — REVIEW MAP